MARK GIBBARD SSJE

Twentieth-Century
Men of Prayer

SCM PRESS LTD

334 01706 8

First published 1974
by SCM Press Ltd
56 Bloomsbury Street London WC1
Fifth impression 1980

Printed in Great Britain by
Richard Clay (The Chaucer Press) Ltd
Bungay, Suffolk

Contents

The spiritual guide is not to teach his own way, but to instruct others how they may themselves find out the way proper for them.

Augustine Baker

We do not want to be beginners, but let us be convinced that we will never be anything else but beginners all our life.

Thomas Merton

The more one can focus on the real historical person the more one sees in the concrete whatever is seeable of his spirituality.

Laurence Barmann

The reality of our communion with Christ and in him with one another is the increase of love in our hearts.

William Temple

Preface

A friend of mine, a capable student, broke off his university studies and thumbed his way overland to Nepal, looking for a guru to teach him prayer. Thousands are on the same search, though without my friend's gay and rash abandon.

We have to find our own way. I am now convinced about that. For some of us our old ways of prayer may have gone dead. And what helps us at one stage may not suit us later on. But there are other ways to explore – often unexpected and inviting ones – even if the going may be tough and sometimes bewildering.

But we needn't be discouraged. Other men and women of our century have found the going hard, but they have come through. We're not expected to imitate precisely any of them; and they worked their way through to astonishingly different types of prayer. Some of these people I have met personally. Each of them has in some way encouraged me. In coming to them again I shall try to spotlight what seems most helpful to us today. I shan't hesitate to say where I disagree with them. In life and in prayer they responded to God's love in such a variety of ways; and you'll get to know them, I hope, still better in their letters and personal writings.

When we go on seeking God, we sometimes have a strange intuition that he is seeking us much more than we are seeking him. There is truth, I think, in the paradoxical words of Pascal, the seventeenth-century mathematician and contemplative: 'You would not have been seeking me unless you had already found me.'

I have as a priest spent a good deal of my thought and time on prayer, but I am no expert. I've a long way to go yet. I'm glad to look at these men and women with you, to see how they develop, and to share with you some of their clues for our own exploration. May we never give up being beginners and explorers.

Oxford, 1974   MARK GIBBARD

I

Charles de Foucauld
and his Fraternities

As a sub-lieutenant in the Fourth Chasseurs d'Afrique, Charles de Foucauld crossed the Mediterranean in a troop-ship and took a stuffy train up to Rétif at an altitude of three thousand feet in Algeria. His mistress had preceded him a week or so before, with her first-class ticket made out as his wife, Mme la Vicomtesse de Foucauld. She charmed and took everybody in – the captain of the boat and colonial officials. Soon the truth came out. Charles was warned, and then his colonel sent for him: 'Either this woman goes or you go.' He replied in effect, 'Then *we* shall go.' He threw up his commission, went back and lived with the girl. He was a man of strong feelings, but above all a man with a fierce will of his own. Later on a fellow-officer described him as plain pig-headed. This was raw material out of which was made a man of prayer.

He was born into an aristocratic family at Strasbourg in 1858. His mother was very devout, but before he was six both his parents had died, and Charles and his younger sister passed into the care of their grandfather. The boy already had a determined will. His grandfather loved him and spoiled him. After the Franco-Prussian war they settled down in Nancy. Charles came under the spell – and this was going to last – of a cousin, eight years older than himself, Marie Moitessier. He disliked study. He wrote home long miserable letters from his Jesuit school in Paris. He entered the Military Academy of St Cyr. He had already lost his boyhood faith – as could easily happen in the sceptical, anti-clerical France of his day. Then from the Cavalry School at Saumur he passed out eighty-seventh out of eighty-seven. All the time – and this was an epoch of courtesans and luxurious living – he was squandering the fortune his grandfather had left him. When his regiment was despatched to Algeria, we have seen what happened. A few months later an insurrection broke out in North Africa. His comrades were fighting; he could not bear to be away from them. He parted from the girl, was re-commissioned – and this time fell in love with Africa.

After this campaign he set his heart on exploring Morocco, then a closed country to Westerners. His indolence was now a thing of the past. He learned to speak Hebrew and Arabic fluently, disguised himself as a rabbi and spent eighteen months lost to the world in Morocco. He had several close shaves with death. Back in Paris he produced a detailed report and was awarded the Gold Medal of the Geographical Society.

He became engaged – for a short time – to the daughter of a distinguished geographer. But Charles' family pressed him to break it off. It was their snobbery; it was the question of the particle. The girl had no aristocratic 'de' in front of her name like de Foucauld. And it was his cousin Marie, who had already become Mme de Bondy, who chiefly talked him out of this romance!

It was also Marie who introduced him to a priest, Abbé Huvelin, urbane and discerning. Charles had been impressed in Morocco by Moslem habits of prayer; and now he was among very intelligent practising Catholics. He would often go into church and pray: 'My God, if you exist, show yourself to me.' He was twenty-eight. After a sleepless night he went to St Augustine's church, where the Abbé was curate. The Madeleine and the Opéra are close by. You can still see the Abbé's confessional on the right-hand side of the church. Charles went up to it. He tells us himself what happened: 'I was asking him for instruction in religion. He told me to kneel and confess, and told me straightaway to receive holy communion.'[1] Clouds of doubt dispersed and faith in God at

[1] Charles de Foucauld, *Ecrits Spirituels* (ed. R. Bazin), de Gigord, Paris 1930, p. 82.

once returned. In a letter to a fellow-officer Charles wrote: 'As soon as I believed that there was a God I was clear that I could then do nothing except live for him. My religious vocation dates from the same hour as my faith.'[2]

Jesus quickly became real to him as a person. Love for Jesus became – and remained – literally the passion of his life. To love Jesus meant for Charles to identify himself with Jesus, in poverty and insecurity sharing with him 'the lowest place that no one could ever take from him'. How to do this, for love of Jesus and his brothers, now became Charles de Foucauld's lifelong exploration.

He thought he would find it by entering a monastery at once. The Abbé made him wait three years. After a pilgrimage to the Holy Land and four retreats to see where his vocation might be, Charles decided on the severest order, the Trappists, as being most likely to provide the 'lowest place'.

The day before he left he received holy communion from Abbé Huvelin, with his cousin Marie, and spent the rest of the day with her. 'How I remember', he wrote, 'your clock which ticked away our last minutes together.'[3] On arriving at the monastery he wrote to her so long a letter that he had no time to write to anyone else. At this monastery of our Lady of the Snows in the Ardèche, he took the name of Frère Marie Albéric and then, at his own request, was sent off to the poorest monastery of the order at Akbès in Syria. He wrote happily from there to Abbé Huvelin: 'I live from one day to the next with our Lord, the most holy Virgin, the saints and with those I love.'[4] His austerity and the deepening of prayer increased his love for his friends all through his life. 'Praying to the Lord for those I love', he said, 'is the chief business of my life,' and he added that he found he now loved them more, not less, than he used to. To his cousin Marie, who wrote to him every week for forty-seven years, he replied: 'How much you

[2] Charles de Foucauld, *Lettres à Henri de Castries*, Grasset, Paris 1938, p. 96.
[3] Charles de Foucauld, *Lettres à Mme de Bondy*, Desclée de Brouwer, Paris 1966, p. 34.
[4] Charles de Foucauld, *Abbé Huvelin: Correspondance inédite*, Desclée de Brouwer, Paris 1957, p. 11.

do constantly for me by your prayer, your letters and your remembrance,' and he thanked her for the rosary she had given him. He kept in warm living touch with the rest of his family.

But quite soon two things troubled him in his love-impelled search for the 'lowest place'. About the first he wrote to the Abbé in his tiny handwriting: 'You express the hope that I now have poverty enough. But no. To the rich we are poor, but we are not poor as our Lord was.' Life at the monastery was too secure. He was sent to pray with a dying peasant. 'What a difference between his hut and where we live,' Charles wrote to Marie. 'I yearn for Nazareth' – for its insecurity. At table he would take only dry bread and water – even on Easter day; and on this point, a fellow-monk reports, he was 'as obstinate as a mule from the Auvergne'. His fierce self-will was not yet mellowed.

Then a second thing troubled him. His superiors wished him to study theology, presumably as a step towards the priesthood. Very reluctantly he began, afraid that if he became a priest people would treat him with respect and he would again lose that 'lowest place' which he was determined to share with Jesus. 'Theology', he wrote to Marie, 'may be admirable; but' – he asked almost mischievously – 'how much did St Joseph know of it?'

Soon he began to dream of gathering companions to found a new order, following Jesus 'in *all* his precepts' – living precariously and simply by their own work; in little 'nests', without monastic hierarchy or distinction between clerics and lay-brothers; with long hours of personal prayer, the rosary and mass, but no elaborate liturgy which outsiders could not understand. This would be the 'lowest place' which he had hoped in vain to find among the Trappists. In this plan we see the seeds of the fraternities which sprang up after his death. But he asked the Abbé: 'Is it a diabolical invention, or is it an idea, an invitation, sent from God?' The Abbé was disappointed that Charles was so restless. He told him to speak again clearly and respectfully to his superiors about his desires. In reply Charles immediately sent the Abbé a detailed new rule he had drawn up, fiercely ascetic: strict enclosure;

4

manual work; perpetual silence; no more than three rooms in a house, no beds, no chairs; only two meals a day, one consisting of soup, the other of bread and water; no Latin office, but again long, long hours of silent prayer.[5]

Abbé Huvelin made a note: 'This rule is impossible, it contains everything except discretion,' and he wrote to Charles: 'What frightens me . . . is to see you founding or thinking of founding anything . . . Do not gather others around you, I beg of you. You need to be protected against this striving towards the infinite, which takes away peace of heart.'[6] This must have been a bitter pill for Charles to swallow. His ferocious determination still needed to be tamed. As a final test the Trappist authorities sent him to Rome to study. At whatever cost he obediently and readily accepted it. But after only three months the Father-General of the Trappists released him from his vows and as a parting-present gave him his own cross.

Now Charles was free to go to Nazareth and take the 'lowest place', where Jesus had taken it. He lived very simply as an odd-job man in a hut just outside the convent of the Poor Clares. He could not lie flat to sleep, the hut was the wrong shape. It has long since fallen to pieces. The Poor Clares have moved out, and I found there four of the community of the Little Sisters, who have since his death drawn their inspiration from him – a French girl, a German, an Italian, a South Vietnamese – living together in simplicity and joy. You can still see the convent chapel and the altar where Charles prayed and almost lived. He dressed very oddly. At first people jeered at him and children threw stones. But he was deeply happy, for he was now literally sharing the lot of the Lord he loved so passionately. This was a turning point. He saw that severe austerity was not the heart of the matter. Love was. A burning human and supernatural love had broken through in his life.

[5] This rule of 1896 for the Little Brothers of the Sacred Heart of Jesus is given in R. Voillaume, *Les Fraternités du Père de Foucauld*, Editions du Cerf, Paris 1946, pp. 156–63; and is summarized in M. Carrouges, *Soldier of the Spirit*, Gollancz 1956, pp. 108–20.

[6] *Abbé Huvelin: Correspondance inédite*, pp. 40–1.

At last he let himself be ordained. Now he felt he could be a priest without losing the 'lowest place' in the world. He said his first mass at the Abbey of our Lady of the Snows in the Ardèche. What a welcome he received from the monks. His sister was there also to receive communion at his hands. Now the door was wide open for him to go back to his beloved Africa.

Commending Charles to the Superior-General of the White Fathers, Abbé Huvelin described him as 'a hard instrument fit for a tough task', and though he had shown in the past 'signs of harshness, there is less of it now'.

His strong feelings, his determined will, are still there, but interpenetrated and transfused by divine love from his experience at Nazareth. He is ready to carry God's love to the ends of the earth. He will preach the gospel – not by sermons, not by instructions, but more and more by *simply loving*. He would continue to live in the 'lowest place' of Nazareth but, as he wrote on the eve of his ordination, 'not where the land is most holy, but where souls are in the greatest need'. He settled down at Beni-Abbès, an Algerian oasis within sight of Morocco. He spent long hours in prayer. He cared himself for the sick and poor. He ransomed a few slaves. He appealed unsuccessfully to the colonial authorities to sweep away slavery. He made friends with the soldiers of the garrison. They served his mass. Occasionally he dined in their mess; as an ex-officer he took the men and the officers as they were. He wished everyone 'to regard him as their brother, *le frère universel*'. He constructed a rough-and-ready monastery and prayed for monks to join him. But in fifteen years only one came and he could not stand the rigour of the life for more than three months, although Charles in his love made minor mitigations for him. The Abbot of our Lady of the Snows, who had a great admiration for Charles, was afraid that 'he might drive his companions mad' by the intense application of mind he would expect of them, 'before causing their death from the excess of his austerities'.

After two years at Beni-Abbès, he was asked to go a thousand miles further into the Sahara. Charles de Foucauld, in spite of his strength of character, often found himself trembling **before** great decisions. He used to say, 'Dread is the sign of duty.' **He** made the journey and soon knew that it was right. For **some** years he divided his time between Beni-Abbès and his **new** hermitage, ministering to the small French garrisons *en route*. But more and more Tamanrasset, on an island of mountains in the heart of the Sahara, became his home. It is here we see the flowering of the man, in and through hardships. The nearest garrison was four hundred miles away. 'For five months', he recorded, 'no news from Europe.' Again and again he wrote in his diary, 'No mass, for I am alone' – and even, 'Christmas: no mass.' This was hard indeed for a man whose life was so centred on this sacrament. Finally exceptional permission came from Rome itself that he could say mass alone, without server or congregation. Then his joy knew no bounds.

Nazareth est partout. You can live the life of Nazareth, he again wrote, everywhere. And here he would live it with its humility and with all its love as a Tuareg among the Tuaregs, this neglected, forgotten people. Their language had not been written before. He translated the gospels for them; he compiled their first grammar and a dictionary in two large volumes; he produced an anthology of their proverbs and love-songs. He had to drive himself hard. He aimed at about eleven hours' study a day. Yet he would cheerfully let himself be interrupted at any moment. Nothing in their lives was too small for him to attend to. He even wrote to his cousin Marie for some black jet dye to help the Tuareg women hide their greying hairs.

He had built himself a hermitage, a long narrow building, about forty feet long by six feet wide, which he appropriately nicknamed 'the frigate'. This was the secret of his life. At one end of 'the frigate' was the altar, made out of packing-cases, and always on it an open Bible, because he met Christ in the sacrament and also in the words of the gospel; he used to spend untold hours at this end of 'the frigate'. At the other end was an open door, where he welcomed with warmth anyone at *any* time. It was said of him, 'It is the heart of Jesus which led him to the heart of all men.'

7

Yet all people, including men of profound prayer, have inconsistencies, pieces which do not fit in; we must not be surprised at this. So we find in Charles de Foucauld an extreme jingoism, extreme even for those colonial days. He acted as a kind of military information-man; French officers called him the *éminence grise* of the Sahara. And of a Moslem 'holy man' who was stirring up trouble he said: 'I would catch the villain, stand him up immediately against a wall and plug twelve bullets into his skin.'

When the 1914–18 war broke out, things were at first fairly quiet in the Sahara. But when in 1916 trouble began he was persuaded to move his hermitage inside a fort at Tamanrasset, fifty feet square, with six-foot thick walls, a ditch around it, a well-barred door – and a store of rifles. One day someone called out that the post had come; and as he put out his hand for his letters, two hostile tribesmen dragged him out and bound him and a third shot a bullet through his head. That is all there is to it – a grain of wheat falling to the ground. That same day, just before he was shot, he had written in a letter to his cousin Marie: 'Our annihilation is the most powerful means we have of uniting ourselves to Jesus and doing good to others.'

His life looked a failure; he left no followers. Then his writings, mimeographed, began to circulate. René Bazin wrote his life. Little groups began to try to live out his early ideas. 'I sow and others will harvest,' he had written. René Voillaume and four other young priests lived an austere Trappist sort of life, as Little Brothers, in a simple monastery at El Abiodh in the desert. When in 1927 Charles de Foucauld's body was moved from distant Tamanrasset to El Goléa, a Christian village in Algeria, a young woman saw a priest dressed like Charles de Foucauld and she asked him who he was. It was Père Voillaume and she was Sister Magdeleine, who had founded the Little Sisters. They had been leading the same life, each quite unaware of the other. By another coincidence Père Voillaume and I happened to meet when we were both visiting the mother-house of the Little Sisters at Tubet, near

Aix-en-Provence. This was after the war, and the Little Brothers and Sisters, following de Foucauld's later insights, had by then moved out into the dechristianized slums of the west and the poorest parts of the third world. Père Voillaume's writings, especially his *Seeds of the Desert*,[7] interpret Charles de Foucauld to us and guide these fraternities.

They live in their small groups of three, four or five. However poor their housing, they keep one room as a tiny chapel, where the holy sacrament is reserved. I remember staying with the Brothers in Marseilles, near an oil refinery where they worked. The smell, the noise, the locality appalled me. They had one room downstairs with a notice on the door: 'Come in without knocking.' Two slept on camp-beds under the stairs; there was one small room upstairs besides the little chapel. In the morning they had reflection on the gospel and mass. When they came home from work, dressed like other workers in their locality, they had an hour of silent prayer – they just sat still for an hour. At first I thought I could never pray in a place like that. But soon – I can't explain it – I felt I wanted to pray more I think than I had ever prayed in my life. It was an extraordinary experience. Perhaps it was I felt so surrounded by people who needed prayer. Perhaps I began to realize that, unless you pray, you cannot expect to be changed into a channel of God's love to others.

Novices for so demanding a life need to be thoroughly trained and tested. I once stayed in a noviciate of theirs on a rocky island off the coast of Brittany. They ran a farm with a few sheep. In the silence and total lack of comfort, there was a sense of belonging to one another and of the challenge of the unexpected – even to going out in a boat to rescue a stubborn sheep from a rock, about to be submerged in a high tide. In all their fraternities there is poverty, not a grim stinginess, but a poverty 'gentle, tender towards suffering, glad and openhearted, and always ready to give or lend'.

The day I left, one of the novices was going to hitch-hike

[7] René Voillaume, *Seeds of the Desert*, Burns & Oates 1955; and Anthony Clarke Books 1972: shortened version of the original French, *Au Coeur des Masses*, Editions du Cerf, Paris 1950.

across France on his way to a major noviciate in Charles de Foucauld's Africa. From there novices visit his original hermitages. They go off on trek in the immensity of the Sahara and spend a week's solitude in a cave on iron rations. We can feel what it is like from Carlo Carretto's *Letters from the Desert*. He was a gifted leader in Catholic Action, who has found his vocation with the Little Brothers in the Sahara. There they acquire a toughness, the mark of the desert.

Then they are moved on to a working fraternity, so they are tested by the hard conditions in which they will live in the future. Afterwards all, laymen as well as priests, go to a house of study. They have come to see that theological study, as Abbé Huvelin reasoned with Charles, will not rob them of the 'lowest place', but will give a firmer foundation to their life of prayer and love.

How these fraternities have grown! Over two hundred Brothers of twenty or so nationalities in fraternities in thirty countries – America and South America, Europe, Africa, the Middle East, Pakistan, India, Korea, Japan and Vietnam. The Little Sisters, like those I came across at Nazareth, are even more widespread – over a thousand of them of fifty different nationalities.

Charles de Foucauld's inspiration for the life of prayer extends far beyond his fraternities into the world of today. He never set out to be a teacher of prayer. Most of what he wrote were masses of intimate notes intended for his own eyes. This makes him more valuable for us. He leaves us to work it out for ourselves. The art of prayer is that there is no art.

His whole life speaks and says that prayer is of *supreme* importance. It can keep us in touch with God, the Love that stands at the heart of reality. When the great breakthrough comes to him at Nazareth, what does he tell us? He writes – but we must not take him too rigidly – that the Christian's prayer should normally be of three kinds: spoken words of prayer, contemplative praying and meditation.

He reminds us first that we shall never grow up out of our spoken words of prayer and leave them behind us – intercession, thanksgiving, prayers together with others. But we have to use all our wits and all our imagination to prevent these becoming mere habits, formalities or even boredom.

Secondly, he lays special stress on some kind of contemplative praying: 'thinking of God with love', he calls it and adds, 'The more one loves, the more one prays.' He himself focused his mind and heart on our Lord most often by kneeling silent before the holy sacrament. But there are many other ways, as we shall see, and each of us needs to explore for himself. Charles de Foucauld maintains – and I agree – that this kind of contemplative praying helps to keep our other prayers alive.

Thirdly, his love of Jesus impels him to reflect *daily* on the gospels, so as to follow Jesus as literally as possible and to share his sufferings. It is like the daily dripping of water, he says, which wears away the stone. We can see the logic of this, but each of us must have his own priorities. Writing down our meditations may help us to be practical and systematic but, like Charles, we must keep such writing absolutely to ourselves – or it may well become a self-conscious pose. There is nothing morbid in what he writes: he mentions past faults only to rejoice in forgiveness; he makes resolutions for the day to express gratitude and confidence. His occasional naivety, his literalism, are part of his special vocation. Yet a literal following of Jesus at times might be no bad thing for many of us. We will look at this again later in the book.

If these kinds of prayer in our lives are genuine, there will almost certainly be – whatever temperaments initially are – some overflowing of real warm love into others' lives: *'pas trace de cette charité froide et distante'* – no trace of that cold and distant charity, as Charles de Foucauld would say.

But it is often hard work to learn to pray, as it is to learn really to love. Don't let us fool ourselves that it is going to be easy. It is hard work – and long work. Let us take it one day at a time and never be discouraged. 'C'est l'oeuvre d'une vie à recommencer chaque matin.' It is the work of a lifetime to begin afresh every morning.

2

Friedrich Von Hügel — Scholar

One of my closest friends gave me, when I was a student, a book which I shall always treasure. It introduced me to just the man I needed. Charles de Foucauld would at that stage of my life have scared me off by his intensity. The book was the *Selected Letters* of Friedrich von Hügel. At that time I was very much wanting to pray, because I sensed that somehow this would help me to understand and help others. But I couldn't pray with much conviction because, although I was studying for the priesthood, I was worried by doubts. Had psychology undermined belief in God? Did the New Testament give us reliable evidence? Was Jesus really what Christians had believed him to be?

And here was a scholar, who had with obvious thoroughness and integrity worked his way through such problems. In these letters you can also watch him growing in prayer and in love, becoming more and more sensitive to others' needs.

I am far from being the only one he helped. Bishop Christopher Butler has said that it was von Hügel who brought him through his tangle of philosophical difficulties at Oxford and helped him to become 'a convinced and open-minded Christian'.[1] Although von Hügel died in 1925, there is about him a contemporary feel – his scientific, empirical outlook, his

[1] From Bishop Butler's estimate of von Hügel in J. P. Whelan, *The Spirituality of Friedrich von Hügel*, Collins 1971, p. 11. For a brief treatment of the intellectual problems mentioned, perhaps I might refer to a small book of mine, *Dynamic of Love*, A. R. Mowbray 1974.

respect for the autonomy of secular studies, his concern for contemplation and for the transcendent. So it does not surprise me that large and detailed studies have quite recently been published about him – Lawrence Barmann's *Baron Friedrich von Hügel and the Modernist Crisis in England* and J. P. Whelan's *The Spirituality of Friedrich von Hügel*.

Perhaps the distinctive clue which Friedrich von Hügel offers us is that we must not be narrowly religious nor turn a blind eye to intellectual problems. We may perhaps only be able to come to partial or provisional solutions. And that is quite enough at least to start with. But not to face up to these difficulties is to run the risk of building a house on sand.

Baron von Hügel was a slow maturer; he did not produce his first book until he was fifty-six. He had grown by facing up to rough weather. Had there been psychologists in his youth, they would have found him an intriguing study.

One of the truths he helps us to grasp is how deep our roots need to go. 'How poor and thin a thing is all purely personal religion' he used to say. 'Religion to be deep and rich must be historical.'[2]

He was rooted in history. His title, Baron of the Holy Roman Empire, came to him from his father, who had actually fought for Austria against Napoleon. After he came out of the army, his father was engaged to a charming Hungarian countess of nineteen. But the romance was broken off. He took it very hard and spent six years travelling round the world to recover. He came back and married a Scots girl, a Presbyterian, later converted to Catholicism, thirty-five years younger than himself. Friedrich was born in 1852 at Florence, the first of three children of this unusual match. The family soon moved to Brussels, where his father became Austrian minister for seven years, and on his retirement they settled in Devon. Friedrich never went to any school or university. Who knows, this may have been an advantage? At any rate he was never, as Ivan Illich would say, 'flattened out' by formal education. Neither was he cured of his obscure prolix style, nor of

2 Gwendolen Greene (ed.), *Letters from Baron Friedrich von Hügel to a Niece*, J. M. Dent 1928, p. xiv.

13

'preciousness' in some of his personal writings. But he is too great a man for such faults to put us off reading him.

He was a gifted linguist, a voracious reader, a man of far-flung interests. He systematically studied geology, for example, with a Quaker geologist and was always grateful for this insight into natural science. Years later he wrote to his Jesuit friend, George Tyrrell: 'I am fifty-seven and I've treated myself to a birthday present. I've bought myself a new geological hammer. So expect to tramp about with me to gravel pits and quarries, please.'[3]

He was as a young man – so his letters show – difficult, obstinate and not particularly religious; he doubted the value of prayer and much else. Then his father died suddenly on his way to revisit Austria. During a year in Vienna Friedrich, now seventeen, caught typhoid. This left him deaf and subject to nervous troubles for the rest of his life. At this same time he came through a spiritual crisis – it is not clear what it was – with the help of Father Hocking, a Dominican. This began to transform his character and prepared him for his life-work. He called it his 'first conversion'.

He married Lady Margaret Herbert when he was twenty-one. They were very much in love, but at first, owing to nervous troubles on both sides, it was rather a strange marriage. They had three daughters. They entertained in cultured Roman Catholic circles. One friend was W. G. Ward, an Oxford don converted to Catholicism, but so extreme that he used to say that he would like to find a papal encyclical on his breakfast table each morning delivered with *The Times*. Baron von Hügel also knew Cardinal Newman, but could not discuss matters with him; the ageing Cardinal had become, he said, like a nervous old lady, hurt and disappointed with anyone who did not agree with him.

But at this stage of his life von Hügel needed someone to talk to – and not an extremist. His faith was deepening, and he longed to communicate it to the new world of his day, a world being shaped by modern science and critical historical studies.

[3] M. D. Petre, *Autobiography and Life of George Tyrrell*, Arnold 1912, ii, p. 97.

So he gradually became a central figure in (what came to be known as) the Catholic Modernist Movement; and, since at first it had few sympathizers in England, he was soon closely linked with Catholics of a similar spirit on the continent, especially in France.

Von Hügel grew through his friendships. There was Professor Duchesne, a pioneer in modern, critical methods. a Catholic historian with an impish tongue, who called the old-fashioned Archbishop of Paris 'that mitred sacristan'. More important was Abbé Huvelin who, as we have seen, proved to be so perceptive a guide also for Charles de Foucauld. So momentous was von Hügel's meeting with the Abbé that he called it his 'second conversion'. He treasured some of the Abbé's sayings. They tell us a great deal about von Hügel – and perhaps they deserve our spotlight:

> Prayer will be for you, rather a state (of mind) than a precise and deliberate act.
> Truth is for you a luminous point which little by little loses itself in the (surrounding) darkness.
> There is no more profound or more dangerous enemy to Christianity than anything which shrinks it and makes it narrow.[4]

Then there was Abbé Loisy, a radical scholar both in the Old and New Testaments. Von Hügel himself was already studying Hebrew. Loisy was bold enough to take on single-handed the world-famous liberal Protestant Professor Harnack of Berlin. But Loisy was treated so unimaginatively and so harshly by his own church that he appeared to be very far from orthodox belief, though he remained a man of religion, and von Hügel never gave him up.

Another friend was the young Jesuit, George Tyrrell, brought up a Dublin Protestant, next an exotic Anglo-Catholic, then a Roman Catholic. He resolved – on the advice of a Catholic landlady, it is said – to try his vocation with the Jesuits; and he described himself as 'an ignorant and drunken navigator who got his vessel into the right port by a mere

[4] Friedrich von Hügel, *Selected Letters*, J. M. Dent 1927, pp. 58–63.

15

fluke'.[5] But once a Jesuit he set out seriously to explore, and to help others to explore, the life of prayer. This is how Baron von Hügel came to ask his help for Gertrude, his eldest daughter. Her father had apparently plunged her into stress and doubt by being over-eager to share his theological problems with her. He was at this period overpowering. Father Tyrrell advised him: 'If you want your daughter's company, you must shorten your steps and walk slowly.'[6] The Baron learned this lesson – and much more – from Father Tyrrell.

But the Roman Catholic authorities came down more and more heavily on the Modernists. Tyrrell according to his temperament struck out polemically and was excommunicated two years before his death in 1909. Von Hügel was in danger himself for a time; but he had come to distinguish between two kinds of modernism. One is the never-ending task of interpreting our faith to the contemporary world. The other maintained that it was unnecessary either to accept even a hard core of events in the gospels as historically proven, or to believe in a God in any sense transcendent and distinct from the world, but only in God immanent in the universe. This kind of modernism in effect substituted pantheism for the gospel. Von Hügel had been drawn towards the first, historical half of it, but never to the second, pantheistic part. And now he took his own warning. Yet he remained to the end a modernist of the first kind. 'When I cease to take in new ideas', he said to Dr John Oman the Presbyterian scholar at Cambridge, as he stepped into his study, 'call in the undertaker.'

All through these years of conflict he had been preparing for his greatest book and for his life-task. It started accidentally. He had picked up a book for his own reading one day, a life of St Catherine of Genoa, a married woman, a medieval mystic. It struck sparks on his anvil. He spoke about it and was asked to write an article on her life for the *Hampstead Annual*. To ask him for an article was like putting a cup under the Niagara. It ended as over eight hundred pages in two volumes. It went round to six publishers. At long last one of his friends per-

[5] Petre, op. cit., i, p. 99.   [6] *Selected Letters*, p. 9.

suaded J. M. Dent & Co. to take it. This was his *Mystical Element in Religion*. Archbishop William Temple called it the most significant theological work in the first half of this century. It is a laborious work, but through it he found his vocation as guide, philosopher and friend to all kinds of people inside the church and outside.

He had a profound influence on some of the greatest scholars of his day. Edwyn Bevan spoke of 'the divine fire' which seemed to fill von Hügel and his 'passionate sense of the reality of God, which broke forth in volcanic utterance'.[7] The liberal Jewish scholar, Claude Montefiore, said that the Baron's books 'great as they are, were but a fraction of the man' and 'for souls such as his, one seems to need God to account for them'.[8]

Evelyn Underhill, married, agnostic, returned to faith in God through a study of mysticism, then found this faith marvellously enriched under the guidance of von Hügel. She wrote:

> When I went to the Baron he said I wasn't much better than a Unitarian. Somehow by his prayers or something, he compelled me to experience Christ. He never said anything more about it – but I know humanly speaking he did it. It took about four months – it was like watching the sun rise very slowly – then suddenly one knew what it was.[9]

Von Hügel was a gentle guide, he knew how to listen, how to understand, but he was never 'soft'. 'You should see my old man dressing me down,' Evelyn Underhill wrote to a friend. Thanks to the training received from him, she became herself a trusted spiritual guide.[10]

His *Letters to a Niece* show how thoroughly he helped Gwendolen Plunket Greene, rather a superficial Anglican, another married woman. He wanted her to be not a 'spectacled

[7] Ibid., p. 35.
[8] Ibid., p. 36.
[9] M. Cropper, *Evelyn Underhill*, Longmans 1958, p. 98.
[10] Works of Evelyn Underhill include *Mysticism*, Methuen 1904 (14th edition 1942); an early work which made her name: *Worship*, Nisbet 1936 (and Fontana 1963); perhaps her most mature work. *The Spiritual Life*, Hodder & Stoughton 1937; four broadcast talks.

blue-stocking' but a 'persevering, balanced, genial, historical Christian'. So the parcels of books he sent to her with notes covered the Latin classics, the Latin Fathers of the Church, the Greek classics. And she was already forty! They read as well the English poets from Caedmon to Browning. They were just starting on Indian religions at the time of the Baron's death. Yet his letters were very down to earth. She was going to move house – 'to pack, pack and unpack, unpack for a fortnight'. Von Hügel said that nothing, not even holy communion, could unite her more closely to God and help her to grow in Christian character than these dreary stretches of life, when necessity and duty require them, provided she did *each* thing as it came 'with heart and intention turned to God'.

No one seemed outside the range of his care. He wrote on similar lines a series of letters to a girl at school. He told her that nothing at all has so bad an effect on us as *'sulking through the inevitable'*.[11] He found time to see twice a week Henri, a French boy of ten who lived opposite, and prepare him for the sacraments. He showed him how to think out his special intentions before mass, how to make his thanksgiving afterwards. He gave him a Greek Testament as the best book to strengthen and stretch them both; and when Henri was eighteen the Baron sold his gold watch-chain to buy him a souvenir of their 'happy hours' together. Once when a parlour-maid of the von Hügel's spoke well at a meeting of the Catholic Evidence Guild, the Cardinal complimented her and asked how she had learned all this. 'Your Eminence,' she replied, 'it's the Baron who teaches me.'

He had of course his limitations. He was almost too proud of his adopted country. During the South African war he was strongly anti-Boer. He maintained that no imperial power cared more than the British did for subject people. He could not see the need for social change in Britain in the opening decades of this century. With all his care for prayer and for the eucharist, he never really saw the eucharist as a community meal from which radiated daily prayer and loving service. He sometimes looked at the cross – without the over-

[11] *Selected Letters*, p. 180 (his italics).

flowing joy of Easter. He would have been fascinated by Taizé fifty years after his death, but he would not have understood it; nor would most of the Taizé brothers understand his philosophical and theological problems.

Yet in his last years how much his help meant to so many in 'the life of prayer'. What this phrase means, as he said, is not easy to analyse – and we need to recall his words again and again. 'Like all living realities, *living religion* possesses a sovereign spontaneity and rich simplicity which seem to render all attempts at an analysis an insult.'[12] It is his characteristic method to begin not with man, nor with the nature of man's relation to God, but with God himself. He affirms that 'God is a stupendously rich Reality,'[13] We are taken at once beyond that naivety of much Christian teaching about God, which has sometimes made so many of us dubious about prayer. The immensity of the universe gives us, von Hügel declares, a *glimpse* of the grandeur of God and his action. Yet far, far more of the wonder of God is disclosed in the life and passion of Jesus Christ. But God is yet more, more even than could be revealed through the human nature of Christ. God is the Beyond. Not only supreme over all, God is also in all. 'God is *near*', von Hügel says to his niece. 'He is no use unless he is near. God's otherness and difference and his nearness. You *must* get that.'[14] Further, God is always the initiator, the awakener—his love awakens our love – the ultimate inspirer even of all that seems most deep and original in us. To him be all adoration and praise.

This authentic prayer and worship should interpenetrate our whole lives. Baron von Hügel saw his task – so Evelyn Underhill truly discerned – as '*arousing the deepest reality of man to the overwhelming Reality, the richness and attraction of God*'.[15]

[12] Friedrich von Hügel, *Eternal Life*, Clark 1913, p. 395.
[13] Friedrich von Hügel, *Essays and Addresses*, J. M. Dent 1926, ii, pp. 217–42. This was of such influence that it was published separately as *The Life of Prayer*, J. M. Dent 1927.
[14] Greene, op. cit., p. xxxi.
[15] Evelyn Underhill, *Mixed Pasture*, Methuen 1933, p. 233 (my italics).

This meant that man's response to God – von Hügel emphasized repeatedly – must first be personal and direct; secondly, must include interests not directly religious, like his own study of geology; and, thirdly, must be corporate.[16]

First, there must be a *personal* life of prayer, an existential relationship with God. 'My soul is athirst for God': this, von Hügel would say, is part of being truly human. In sharp contrast to this many people have said in recent years that the real way to show your desire for God, your love for God, is to involve yourself in the service of your neighbours, particularly the underprivileged. There is of course much truth in this view, as the New Testament makes clear. But I think it has been pressed too far – in over-compensation for past neglect of our social responsibilities. Perhaps I may suggest a comparison. A great deal of a man's love for his wife and hers for him is shown in their care for their family and for their neighbours. But that surely is not the whole of their love. There is also the essential direct giving of their love to each other. Indeed this expression of mutual love enriches all their love and creates more for others. So our desire for God himself, our direct giving of love to him in response to his love, our adoration, is essential to an authentic life of prayer. It in turn should both enrich our love for others and purify it from possessiveness. As Henri Bremond, one of the Baron's friends, used to say, genuine worship 'disinfects our service from egoism'.

This directness of love and adoration was clear in von Hügel's own life. When he lived in Hampstead, scholars used to come to stay with him, and they would walk on the heath in the afternoon, discussing points of philosophy and theology. On the way back they would slip into a small Roman Catholic church near his home, and one of them has said: 'If you've never seen the massive head of the Baron bowed in adoration, you haven't seen half the man.' Of course I well understand that many people, many Christians, would say that this sort of worship is outside their experience, beyond their under-

---

[16] This is set out most conveniently in Friedrich von Hügel, *Mystical Element in Religion*, J. M. Dent 1933, i, pp. 50–82; ii, pp. 341–96 and *Eternal Life*, pp. 395–6.

standing. Von Hügel in reply would invite them – and this is the aim of this book – to investigate this area of human experience for themselves. 'The spiritual world is a great world of facts,' he wrote, 'and you must learn about it, as you would learn forestry from the forester. After five or six years among trees you will know something about them.'[17] A person without any such experience, he insisted, 'remains or becomes but half a man'.

But he knew by what varied ways people come to this relationship with God. He was certain – he had now learned this lesson – that each one must find, needs to be guided to, the way which suits his own temperament, his own *attrait*. He told his niece that we must be like cows browsing in the meadow, we should take the particular kind of pasture which suits us and just leave the rest – and never snort at or trample on what does not now help us but may help others. For example, he told Evelyn Underhill that although the traditional prayer, the divine office of the church, is of great value to many people, she was *not* to use it. 'The praying of a few psalms, or even only snatches of psalms, is good. But I would not take the recitation of an entire office, however short. Not your *attrait*.' And he was all against picking up an assortment of religious practices from various sources instead of trying to discover a way authentic for oneself. Books like this one need to be read with discrimination. And an experienced guide is often necessary. He said about himself: 'I never learnt anything myself by my own old nose.'

But he was convinced that many people could find, and needed to find, a simple, contemplative kind of praying.

> The happiest and most fruitful moments, those in which our mind expands and grows most are those in which we are unforcedly and massively absorbed in drinking in the contrasts and harmonies, the grand unity in variety, the very presence and spirit of an Alpine upland, or of a river's flowing, or of ocean's outspread, or the Parthenon sculptures, or of Raphael's madonnas . . . When we return to our ordinary physical and mental condition, we do so with an undeniable sense of added strength and youthfulness.[18]

[17] Greene, op. cit., p. xv.
[18] *Mystical Element in Religion*, ii, p. 133.

21

Then, secondly, our life of prayer must be fed by interests *not directly religious*. Otherwise we run the danger of becoming tense and narrow Christians – and this is what puts many enquirers off. Direct times of prayer are the yeast; non-religious activities are the dough, von Hügel used to say. You cannot live on yeast alone. He advised his niece to give an hour and a half daily to her violin practice, even if it meant a little shortening of her time for prayer. He told Evelyn Underhill to visit poor families twice a week, because she seemed sometimes to be too fastidious or too cerebral in her religion. 'It will distribute your blood – some of your blood – from your brain, where too much of it is lodged at present.' To a girl of seventeen, preparing for confirmation, he wrote: 'Love your games, your dancing, your hunting, devote yourself to your studies of history or science and help (in proportion to your special gifts) in social, political, moral questions and necessities . . . *The more varied and vigorous is your general, not directly religious life, the better for your religion.*'[19]

In his own life historical and linguistic studies, besides geology, played this part. He stressed the importance, for everyone who could profit from it, of the discipline of a careful, historical study of the scriptures and Christian documents. This would incidentally help to pare away those accretions, even superstitions, which during the centuries have gathered around the Christian faith, as all other faiths, and so prepare us to commend our faith to the mind and heart of the contemporary world.

Thirdly, he stressed the *corporate* side of the life of prayer, our need to belong to the church. Even though he himself, as we have seen, had great difficulties with his church, came near to being excommunicated and called the church his 'hair-shirt' and his 'deepest pain', yet he never considered leaving it. In spite of its harshness and imperfection, he knew he must live within the life of the church, the life of its ordinary people. Profound man of prayer that he was, he continued to say his rosary daily. He dreaded spiritual pride, any kind of *élitisme*. 'For myself', he said, 'I must remain in the crowd, not only for

[19] Letter quoted in Whelan, op. cit., p. 228.

the crowd's sake but especially for my own.' He knew that the love of God in its breadth and length, height and depth is so immense and many-sided that, as the epistle to the Ephesians says, we can only come to grasp it by sharing in the insights of *all* the faithful (3.17-18). So, Baron von Hügel himself affirmed in his *Mystical Element in Religion*, we are called to be

> a great living cloth of gold with, not only the woof going from God to man and from man to God, but also the warp going from man to man . . . and thus the primary and full Bride of Christ never is, nor can be, the individual man at prayer, but only this complete organism of all faithful people throughout time and space.[20]

His teaching was massive and rich: no wonder that Maude Petre, friend and biographer of Father Tyrrell, though sometimes critical of von Hügel, wrote that when the Baron died 'it was like a mountain range being lifted off the earth'.[21]

[20] *Mystical Element in Religion*, ii, p. 356.
[21] M. D. Petre, *My Way of Faith*, J. M. Dent 1937, p. 256.

3

Simone Weil and Madeleine Delbrêl – in the Social Struggle

Perhaps we need to remind ourselves that we can only pray authentically, if we pray where we are – not where we aren't! Can we be sincerely praying, if we close our ears to the oppressed and underprivileged of the world around us? We may have forgotten how that man of prayer, Isaiah, expressed the Lord's message:

> When you lift your hands outspread in prayer, I will hide my eyes from you.
> Though you offer countless prayers, I will not listen.
> There is blood on your hands...
> pursue justice and champion the oppressed (Isa. 1.15-17).

Simone Weil and Madeleine Delbrêl were women of prayer who both struggled for the suffering and the unjustly treated.

Simone was born in 1909, a doctor's daughter in an affluent apartment, overlooking the Luxembourg Gardens, with a fine view of Paris. Yet 'she had *the poverty of those who seek*' – so a friend summed up her life.[1] Seeking for truth and sharing the hardships of the unjustly treated – these two intertwined concerns traced out her arduous road of prayer to God.

Even as a child during the 1914–18 war she had some of her rations sent to a soldier at the front. She refused to wear stockings in the winter to be like the urchins of Paris. She did this to annoy her parents and also to protest against their comfortable ways. They were fond of her, but in an undemon-

[1] Simone Pétrement, *La Vie de Simone Weil*, Fayard, Paris 1973, ii, p. 403.

strative manner. Her brother was even more brilliant than she was, and she overheard a remark, 'He's a genius, but she's beautiful.' This drove her into a frenzy of intellectualism and into a suppression of her femininity. Her parents were both agnostic Jews. But some of her relations were over-rigid Jews. This put her off all religion, especially Judaism.[2] Little wonder she became, as T. S. Eliot described her, 'a difficult, violent, complex personality'.[3] Neither loving nor believing nor praying were going to come readily to Simone. She said she put the question of God's existence into a corner, until it refused to stay there any longer.

She gained first place in the 1928 entrance examination to the Ecole Normale Supérieure, a top-ranking educational institution in Paris, with Simone de Beauvoir, the future novelist, second. Simone Weil read philosophy, she needed no encouragement to question everything and anything. Life was then Spartan, and students were expected to rise at 5.00 each day except, as a concession to student flesh, on two mornings at 6.00. Charles de Foucauld had been called at his Jesuit school in Paris every morning at 4.50.

Simone was a girl with an incisive mind. She was a great arguer, with a flat, dull voice. She did not know how to dress, and she had no charm for men – in fact they called her 'the categorical imperative in skirts'.

She started her teaching at Le Puy in the Auvergne. She was like one of the outcrops of volcanic rock in that bizarre part of France. She just didn't fit in. She stimulated some of the abler girls, but most of the examination results were poor. Yet what bothered their respectable parents even more was that this odd mistress shouldered a pick to go to break stones along with the unemployed, gave away most of her salary so as to live on the level of their dole, attended their protest

[2] This information about her childhood comes from Père Perrin's preface to his edition of *Attente de Dieu*, La Colombe, Paris 1950, pp. 17–18: unfortunately it does not appear in the English translation, *Waiting on God*, Routledge & Kegan Paul 1951; Fontana 1959 (all following references are to the Fontana edition).

[3] In his preface to Simone Weil, *The Need for Roots*, Routledge & Kegan Paul 1952, p. v.

meetings, and even wasted her time playing cards with them. 'Here comes the Red virgin of the tribe of Levi,' people said, 'preaching the gospel of Moscow.' She never held any teaching post for long, which is not surprising.

She took a year off from teaching to work in three factories in Paris. She did not live with her parents, but by herself in a working-class district. She cared and wanted to share completely the factory workers' life in that decade of long hours and low wages. She was so roughly treated that she said that ever afterwards she felt like a slave branded with a red-hot iron.

Then the Spanish civil war broke out and she went to fight for the Reds. With a rifle she was of more danger to her friends than to her foes. She was always clumsy, and spilt some hot fat over her legs and so, mercifully, had to be taken to hospital in Barcelona, where her family picked her up and took her back to Paris. Through these tormented years she was seeking and seeking God.

Her family left Paris just before the Nazis took it over. As a Jewess she was now forbidden to teach. They lived in the unoccupied zone of southern France. Here God and prayer came to mean much more to her. She met and became very close to a blind Dominican, Père Perrin in Marseilles, apparently the only priest she ever confided in; and she once told him that she wished that he was a book rather than a man. She used to go to mass, she adored Christ in the holy sacrament, she regarded her self-identification with the poor and ill-treated as a kind of participation in Christ's sufferings. She liked to say the Lord's prayer but in an odd scrupulous way; whenever she was saying it, if her mind wandered, she would go back to the beginning again. She was a strange person – sincere but strange. And she refused for a variety of reasons to be baptized. She felt that she must not separate herself from the left-wing radicals and non-believers. She said she was called to live 'at the intersection of Christianity and all that was non-Christian'.[4]

She worked on a farm, and shared the exhausting labours of harvest. She refused to live in the farmhouse, but went off by

4 *Waiting on God*, p. 42.

herself to a ruined cottage. She ate practically nothing. She was now learning Sanskrit and she even tried – in her rather imperceptive way – to instruct a farm girl in Hindu spirituality.

Her family managed to get a boat to the States and she went with them. But soon she was in England, working for the Free French. She asked to be parachuted into France to share in the dangers of the Resistance. But she was put on to write a report on the possibilities after the war of building up a new France, free from the injustices and poverty of the old France. In it she protested against that too unworldly 'spurious contemplation' so different from her own long search for God: 'It is only through things and individual beings on this earth that human love can penetrate to what lies beyond.'[5]

Her own seeking God was always linked to her care for and her identification with the suffering. She refused to eat any more food than the lowest rations in occupied France. She practically starved herself to death. At last she had to go to hospital and died at a sanatorium in Kent in 1943.

Her life's search for God had been chiefly in darkness. But she has told us of three particular moments of disclosure.[6]

The first was when after her year in the factories she was in a poor fishing village in Portugal. It was full moon. The wives of the fishermen were going in procession among the boats on the beach, carrying candles and singing litanies. She felt at one with these women living a life of poverty and insecurity, and something of the divine broke through to her.

The second was rather more to be expected. She was visiting the little church of St Mary of the Angels within the great basilica at Assisi. She remembered how Francis in self-identification with the poor often prayed just there. And she said: 'I couldn't but go down on my knees for the first time in my life.'

The third started from a visit to the Benedictine monastery of Solesmes for Holy Week in the year before the war began.

[5] *The Need for Roots*, p. 151.
[6] In an autobiographical letter to Père Perrin in *Waiting on God*, pp. 28–48.

She was suffering from migraines, as she did throughout most of her life. She was moved by the liturgy and the singing of the monks. But most important, a guest lent her a book of seventeenth-century English poetry. Some of these poems attracted her at first just as literature. Later that year, as she was reading one of them, something quite unexpected happened to her. She has recorded the moment:

> I thought I was merely reciting it as a beautiful poem, but, without my knowing it, it had the virtue of prayer. It was during one of these recitations that Christ himself came down and took possession of me.[7]

The words she was reading, from George Herbert, were these:

> Love bade me welcome, yet my soul drew back,
> Guilty of dust and sin.
> But quick-ey'd Love, observing me grow slack
> From my first entrance in,
> Drew nearer to me, sweetly questioning
> If I lack'd anything.
> 'A guest', I answered, 'worthy to be here';
> Love said, 'You shall be he'.

Many of us who try to live a life of prayer, experience these times of doubt and obscurity, sometimes at the beginning and often much later on as well.[8] This may be distressing but it is nothing to be too anxious or impatient about. But we should look to see whether we have brought upon ourselves this difficulty in our life of prayer, rather as a couple might examine some problem in their marriage. Our prayer may sometimes seem to go dead, when we are over-worked and run-down in health; or when we are shying away from some intellectual problem instead of facing it; or when we have let our praying – as some people let their personal relationships – become mere routine. Perhaps there is some basic inconsistency in our lives; or we may be obsessed by some fear about the future.

Yet on the other hand it may well be none of these things. It may be just an *unavoidable* 'difficult patch'. We have to deal

---

[7] *Waiting on God*, p. 35 and Pétrement, op. cit., pp. 207–10.

[8] These difficulties are dealt with in rather more detail in my book, *Why Pray?*, SCM Press 1970, pp. 108–15.

with these patches in our personal relationships, and if we find out how to handle them, they may in the end deepen our friendship and love. Similarly these times of doubt and perplexity sometimes refine, mature and deepen our faith and love for God. If only we could remember that God is there all the time – and within us, working within us. Simone Weil knew what such people go through.

> They do not turn to God. How could they do so when they are in total darkness? God himself sets their faces in the right direction. He does not, however, show himself to them for a long time. It is for them to remain motionless and waiting, they know not for what.[9]

And they can take courage from some words of her guide, Père Perrin:

> Whoever makes himself unconditionally open to truth and tries to love his neighbour, his every neighbour, has himself found God and is quite close to seeing God come to him.[10]

But it involves for us as for Simone seeking at the same time both God and the real good of our neighbours.

Madeleine Delbrêl saw this too. She and Simone were living in Paris at the same time. I wonder if they ever met. I would have given a small fortune to hear them talk together. Madeleine became a thorough Catholic; she was, a friend said, 'rooted in the Church at the cross-roads of love'. She learned how without compromise of principle to work with Communists in the social struggle. A Marxist, reviewing her last book, could write in the local Communist weekly: 'You not only worked with the Communists for just causes. You knew how to understand them. We shall not forget you. Thank you, Madeleine.'

Born in 1904, she was the only daughter of a railwayman. He was moved about all over France, so Madeleine's education was, as she said, 'absolutely chaotic'. Her father was self-educated, anti-clerical and atheist. There was no religion in the home, but Madeleine liked to go to church and, when she

[9] *Waiting on God*, p. 162.
[10] *Attente de Dieu*, p. 9 (only in the French edition).

was twelve, made her first communion. Her father was promoted and they came to Paris. Her parents dreamed that Madeleine might become a professional musician. She loved art galleries. She dabbled in philosophy. She wrote poetry and later published a prize volume of her poems. Her father now belonged to a free-thinking circle. They flattered this precocious young girl, and she in turn declared herself an atheist.

But she also became friendly with a group of young people, lively intelligent Catholics. For a short time she was engaged to a young man who talked about the philosophy of St Thomas Aquinas, even while dancing. It was through the influence of this group that she experienced what she called 'a violent conversion following from a reasoned religious search'.[11] She said little about it, but she never looked back and now she began to pray seriously.

> I chose what seemed to me the best way to register my change of perspective. I decided to pray. Previously in reading and reflecting I have found God, but in praying I believe God *found me*.[12]

She never lost her natural gaiety, nor the freshness and joy of her conversion. 'Radiant', people always called her – '*une éblouie de Dieu*'.

She wished to enter a Carmelite convent. But her father lost his sight and lived a more and more irregular life. This was very hard on her mother and it went on for thirty years until both parents died. Madeleine saw she must stay in the world and support her parents; and the carrying of this burden brought to her both the gift of really entering into others' misfortunes and the deepening of her life of prayer.

She came to the conviction that she was called '*to live the gospel in the heart of the world*'.[13] It sounds very much like Charles de Foucauld and his fraternities. She went with two friends, a nurse and a laboratory worker, to live in Ivry, first in a small house by the church, then in a larger house in the

[11] Madeleine Delbrêl, *Nous Autres, Gens des Rues*, Editions du Seuil, Paris 1966, p. 17.
[12] Madeleine Delbrêl, *Ville Marxiste, Terre de Mission*, Editions du Cerf, Paris 1970, pp. 251-2 (italics mine).
[13] *Nous Autres, Gens des Rues*, p. 22.

narrow grim Rue Respail. A heavy forbidding door makes it look like a small factory. But inside there is a warm welcoming home and a long narrow garden with outhouses which have often sheltered refugees. Madeleine trained as a social worker – in not, I think, a very high grade. Then there she lived for over thirty years and there she died in 1964. She said: 'Ivry was my school of applied faith' – and a hard school it was.

At first there was great tension. The local council was dominated by Communists. Catholics were discriminated against in the public services. There were anti-religious demonstrations. In the streets stones were thrown at priests. There were public fights. Catholics from their side boycotted Communist shopkeepers and tried to keep Communists out of the liberal professions.

Then came the great slump and, as in England, there were millions of unemployed. The Communist leader, Maurice Thorez, appealed to all men of goodwill to join together in a Popular Front. Madeleine, with the new liberal Catholic laity and priests, responded. So for thirty years she was very active in the social services of Ivry. She knew exactly what was going on. As secretary of various committees she was an impeccable keeper of minutes.

But she regarded as one of her principal responsibilities keeping open house in Rue Respail. Their telephone was always ringing. People came and went all day and almost all night. There she was – slim, agile, charming, but with an air of decision and energy. She welcomed you with a smile. Her large shining eyes seemed to take you in with whatever your joys or fears or problems might be. Her very self created an atmosphere of confidence, strength and gaiety. No wonder people of all sorts came. She knew that her secret was in prayer. But how in that situation and among people who had lost all sense of God, could she maintain her life of prayer? That is a problem not only for Madeleine.

How difficult it was for her and her friends to find time for prayer. And even when there was time, how difficult often to summon up the will and energy to pray. On the other hand, they knew some people who said that the serving of others was itself their praying, and that was *all* the praying they needed to do. And these people interpreted in this way the old saying 'To work is to pray'. But Madeleine thought that was a misinterpretation. Certainly it would not do for her and for her friends. They knew their own weaknesses too well. They were sure that 'prayer is the energy of action'[14] – and so indispensable for them. They also discovered how easily in our service of others we become patronizing, possessive, quickly discouraged, easily hurt – all symptoms of egoism. And Madeleine was convinced that 'prayer liberates us from our egoism' – we must find, she said, what kind of prayer has this effect for us. They knew that the quality of their service deteriorated, unless they took time *from* service and gave it *to* prayer. It might have to be a fairly short time of prayer, but it would be taking time 'from the useful for the more useful'.[15]

But they did not fence off their times of prayer during the day. They had no timetable of prayers, nor an oratory, as even the Little Sisters of Charles de Foucauld have. They were ordinary people in the world, showing *how* hard-pressed people in the world can pray.

What matters in prayer is not length but love, not a system but desire for God. Love generates desire, and desire makes us – in intercession and in every kind of prayer – 'meet with the living God, the living Christ'. A loving desire for him makes us turn to him almost spontaneously in the minutes while we wait to buy a ticket, to get on a bus, for a phone to be free – just as our thoughts go to those we love. This is *la prière à vif*. Love makes us ready for such moments, so that we don't waste them by useless day-dreaming, by being beguiled by advertisements or worse by futile grumbling to ourselves. This does not mean being tense, never having a moment for ourselves, but

[14] Madeleine Delbrêl, *Joie de Croire*, Editions du Seuil, Paris 1969, p. 123.

[15] Madeleine Delbrêl, *Communautés selon l'Evangile*, Editions du Seuil, Paris 1973, p. 155. This book shows how her informal fraternity differs from religious communities. Her fraternity continues today with about twenty members in three centres in Paris and two in Africa. They meet annually for conference and retreat.

always being open to One whom we love. Prayer is not a drill, it is love – and love always finds a way. We cannot go off to a desert for our retreat. 'A journey of five stations in the metro at the end of the day is our desert'; and the noise that really distracts us from prayer is not the rattling of the train, nor the talk of the passengers, but the self-centred rumblings and grumblings in our own hearts.

This is all so obvious. But why don't we pray like that? Often because we treat prayer, as we sometimes treat friendship, just as an ordinary thing which we can take for granted. But 'prayer is', Madeleine reminds us, 'a *gift* of God';[16] and we shall never really pray, unless continually we ask God for his gift of prayer. We need to experience prayer, like love, as a gift every day, a fresh gift, a gift far beyond what we deserve.

If we have this love, we shall find ourselves not only thinking of God frequently during the day, but getting up ten minutes earlier to be alone with him in prayer and spending an hour or so with him on a day off or on holiday. Isn't this what happens when there is love?

To keep love living and growing is, Madeleine says, one of the purposes of the New Testament. She knows of course the value of a small group reading the Bible together. But this cannot take the place of our individual turning to the gospel where we meet the Lord personally – *tête-à-tête*. 'The gospel is a book you pray.' We treasure it, as friends read, re-read and keep their letters to one another.

Although she was so open, so natural, so spontaneous with others, she never watered down her convictions to please them. For it is less than love – to give less than the truth as you have come to see it. She must speak the truth in love – sensitively and humbly – whether to Communists or to other sorts of Christians. Once when Madeleine was at the Ecumenical Institute at Bossey in Switzerland she and members of other churches were each asked to speak about prayer for seven minutes – authentically but non-controversially – with nothing about dogmas or sacraments – how well I know these ecumenical ploys! She reflected and then said that she could not

[16] *Joie de Croire*, p. 217.

quite tie up with their conditions but she would have her seven minutes. I quote her own words but I must abbreviate:

> What is to me most precious in prayer is that I belong to Jesus Christ. I am his – in the Roman Catholic church. I am in her as a cell in a living body. She transmits to me the life of the children of God.
>
> To live as a child of God in Christ means to be with him, to speak with him, to speak with him personally. It is always to be *en famille*, always at home with everybody and at the same time always at home with God.
>
> For me, to pray is to be sharing in the prayer of the church, and the prayer of the church is inseparable from the life of the church, her sacramental life, the eucharist, the supper of the Lord. With him she makes all one.[17]

And so Madeleine went on. She drew other people out. The whole session came alive. How much more authentic and loving than the attitude 'I don't want to hurt your feelings, but . . .'

It was her experience that she could not really serve the world and live the gospel, unless her roots were deep in the Christian community. 'You can't live the life of a realistic gospel in an abstract church.'[18]

[17] *Joie de Croire*, pp. 211–12.
[18] *Nous Autres, Gens des Rues*, p. 34.

4

Dietrich Bonhoeffer – Man Transformed

Dietrich Bonhoeffer, a contemporary of Simone Weil and Madeleine Delbrêl, I had long admired as a man of immense courage, executed by Hitler at the very end of the war; and also as a theologian, whose cryptic jottings in prison started a post-war theological revolution: but I had not realized what a profound man of prayer he eventually became until I joined an Oxford seminar on prayer in 1964. Mary Bosanquet, one of its members, whose book *The Life and Death of Dietrich Bonhoeffer* was published four years later, brought us some extracts of his unpublished papers on prayer. This started me off.

I was entranced by the deeper insight these writings gave into Bonhoeffer, though much about him remains elusive still. It seems to me that largely by his perseverance in prayer he became, through the Spirit, a man transformed. 'Prayer if it is real', Douglas Steere, an American Quaker friend of mine has said, 'is an acknowledgment of our finitude, our need, *our openness to be changed, our readiness to be surprised*, yes astonished by the "beams of love".'[1] That to me is Bonhoeffer's life in its development.

Dietrich, born in 1905, was one of eight children; first, there were three boys who formed a group of their own; next, two sisters; then Dietrich and his twin sister; and finally the youngest sister. Dietrich became – and remained almost all through his life – a rather reticent, odd-man-out.

His father was professor of psychiatry at the university of

[1] Douglas V. Steere, in his foreword to Thomas Merton, *Contemplative Prayer*, Darton, Longman & Todd 1973, p. 8.

Berlin – and one of the old school. Eberhard Bethge, Dietrich's intimate friend, nephew by marriage and biographer, wrote that the old father turned his university post 'into a bastion against the invasion of Freud's and Jung's psychoanalysis'.[2] This attitude passed on from father to son, so Dietrich, in spite of all his own experience of counselling others, could write of psychotherapists as those who 'set themselves to drive people to inward despair' and 'then the game is in *their* hands'.[3] The father, as we might have guessed, was a man of few words; with a mere look he could, and did, deflate people. Meals were rather formal; at table the children were to address their words to their parents; in general they were to be seen, but not heard. In this family it was 'not done' to be emotional or to show pain. Years later during the heavy raids on Berlin Dietrich remarked, 'Fright is something we ought to be ashamed of.'[4] They were brought up conscious of their privileged position with a disdain for those who could not measure up to their own high standards. No wonder that, as Eberhard Bethge admits, many people thought Dietrich haughty.

His mother was a warmer personality. She and her husband were very fond of each other. She knew how to get her way with charm. She sang with enthusiasm if not accuracy. She was a woman of courage. In the appalling conditions near the end of the war, when almost seventy, she wrote to Dietrich, 'We are staying in Berlin, come what may.'[5] She gave all her children their first schooling. In her youth she had spent some months with the Moravian Brethren at Herrnhut. But her religious enthusiasm went below the surface after her marriage. The family seldom if ever went to church. But the children said grace before meals, they had evening family prayers and much carol-singing at Christmas and the New Year. The father was present, but he was of a sceptical frame of mind and used to say humorously, 'I understand nothing of it.'

In this non-church family Dietrich decided before he was

[2] Eberhard Bethge, *Dietrich Bonhoeffer*, Collins 1970, p. 11.

[3] Dietrich Bonhoeffer, *Letters and Papers from Prison*, The Enlarged Edition, SCM Press 1971, p. 326 (my italics). All following references are to this, the definitive edition.

[4] Ibid., p. 146.   [5] Ibid., p. 404.

fourteen to become a minister and a theologian. He never said why – this is part of his reticence – but he never swerved from his choice. His family tried to laugh him out of it, saying that the church was dull and boring. 'In that case', he replied, 'I shall reform it.' It is possible that he made this choice in order to outshine his three brothers. They were all old enough to be called up for the first world war, and they were all absorbed in natural science, which meant nothing to him. He was perhaps determined to do something which they could not. Anyway, Eberhard Bethge said, 'Because he was lonely, he became a theologian and because he was a theologian he was lonely.'[6] A little later a master at school asked him what he wished to study. Dietrich quietly answered 'theology' and flushed. It was partly embarrassment and partly vanity at attempting something unusual. But he meant what he said; he promptly started Hebrew at school. Yet there was no narrowing of his interests; he sang, he danced, he played the piano with skill, he hiked, he went to the opera. He had time and energy for everything. He worked with incredible speed and concentration. He set out on his career as a theologian efficiently and from a worldly base.

He left home for the first time at seventeen to read theology at Tübingen, his father's university. After two terms he visited Italy. Lutheran as he always was, he loved Rome – 'one of my favourite parts of the world', as he called it twenty years later writing from a prison cell. Two things struck him like a revelation, which he never lost – a vision of the universality of the church and the glory of liturgical worship.

He came back and on Berlin station gave his twin sister a guitar and a kiss – rather an event for such an emotionally reserved family. She had just become engaged to a brilliant young lawyer, a Jew. Dietrich now lived at home and studied at Berlin university, maintaining a theological line of his own. Afterwards he spent a year as assistant pastor in Barcelona, returning to Berlin to be assistant lecturer. Then he went for a year to the Union Theological Seminary in New York. He wrote back to Germany: 'The students have not the faintest

[6] Bethge, op. cit., p. 23.

notion of what dogmatic theology is about!'[7] He made friends with one of the then few black students at 'Union' and came to know Harlem from the inside.

He was back in Germany before Hitler came to power on 30 January 1933. The next day Dietrich broadcast on 'Changes in the Concept of a Führer'. Before he had finished, he was cut off. The Nazis now clearly had their eye on him. Partly to make the German situation known abroad, he spent two years in charge of a Lutheran church in London.

In Germany the division was hardening between the majority of the Protestants who did not oppose Hitler, and a minority, the Confessing Church, who did. Dietrich was now called back to start an illegal underground seminary to train young pastors for this Confessing Church. He saw clearly that these men would need a courage and a determination which could only come to them from God through an authentic life of prayer.

And something – or possibly a series of things – had happened to him. His reticence veils what it was. He alluded to it in a letter about his ministry to a girl to whom he was very close at that time:

> I plunged into work in a very unchristian way. An ambition that many noticed in me made my life difficult . . . Then something happened, something that has changed and transformed my life to the present day . . . I had often preached, I had seen a good deal of the Church, and talked and preached about it – but I had not yet become a Christian . . . I know that at that time I turned the doctrine of Jesus Christ into something of personal advantage to myself . . . I pray to God that that will never happen again. Also I had never prayed, or prayed very little . . . Then the Bible, and in particular the Sermon on the Mount, freed me from all that. It was a great liberation.[8]

The challenging call had come. The 'something' had happened. The years of preparation had been building up to this moment.

[7] Quoted in Mary Bosanquet, *The Life and Death of Dietrich Bonhoeffer*, Hodder & Stoughton 1968, p. 83.
[8] A letter from Finkenwalde dated 27.1.36, quoted by Bethge, op. cit., pp. 154 f.

But one thing remained before he returned to Nazi Germany. He decided to visit three Anglican monastic communities for men. Brief as these visits had to be, they affected him profoundly like his earlier visit to Rome. In these communities he now glimpsed what he was seeking for the next *stage* of his life and ministry – men living together in fraternal love and in a disciplined life of prayer – the regular rhythm of worship, the meditative singing of the psalms, the silence and meditation. He knew that both he and these young pastors needed this discipline of prayer.[9]

Soon he was with his students at Finkenwalde, a few miles inland from the Baltic. They took over a country house, once a school, now derelict. He and his students quickly had it in some sort of order. There was vigorous theological work, singing, piano-playing and all sorts of recreation. Bonhoeffer was in everything.

What the students were not at all ready for was to be plunged at once into what they called Bonhoeffer's 'new style of monasticism'. Of course he gave the reason why and outlined it as a book, *Life Together*, when, two years later, the seminary was closed down by the police. It is a concentrated book, but well worth reading. In those formative years, each day there was half an hour's worship first thing in the morning and last thing at night. And after the night worship there was silence.

The worship consisted of psalms, Bible reading, hymns and some free prayer, which was usually led with great sensitivity by Bonhoeffer himself. He was ready for flexibility, but commended this basic plan – for the prayers of a family or of a group of friends or ministers. He stressed that the Christian does not really pray alone, but always in the companionship of his fellow-believers, and also in union with the risen Christ, who 'ever lives to make intercession for us'.

At Finkenwalde he also insisted on the Catholic tradition of praying through the entire psalter, which he called 'the great school of prayer'. Christ on earth prayed the psalms. Through

[9] On these visits to Anglican communities, see the article by J. Rieger in *I Knew Dietrich Bonhoeffer* ed. W. D. Zimmermann and R. Gregor Smith, Collins 1966, pp. 97 f.

the same praises and prayers we can identify ourselves with the glorified Christ and so, with him, intercede for the world.

Essential to their worship also was to read, not only those short passages that appealed to them, but right through the scriptures continuously. They had to find themselves, he said, beside their spiritual ancestors in *all* their struggles and doubts. 'Only in so far as we are *there*, is God with us today.'[10]

They received holy communion, not very frequently, but after careful preparation and mutual reconciliation. Bonhoeffer declared that this 'has been the chief means of bringing us together'.[11] He urged, though did not force, the practice of individual confession to some other member of the seminary.

> Christ gave his followers the authority to hear the confession of sin and forgive sin in his name . . . Christ became our Brother in order to help us . . . Now our brother has been given to us to help us. He hears the confession of our sins in Christ's stead and he forgives our sins in Christ's name. He keeps the secret of our confession, as God keeps it. When I go to my brother to confess, I am going to God.[12]

Bonhoeffer went to Eberhard Bethge, who was now one of his seminarians, for his own confession.

After a time he set up an inner community, a *Bruderhaus*, a House of Brothers, who shared all their resources, would go wherever their help was needed, but would be permanently based on Finkenwalde. This looked even more monastic, but Bonhoeffer was emphatic that this was 'not the seclusion of a monastery, but a place of the deepest inward concentration for service outside'.[13]

What caused the greatest consternation – indeed almost a riot – was Bonhoeffer's insistence on half an hour's silent meditation after breakfast on scripture – and often on the same passage day after day for a week. He made clear that this was not Bible study, but its indispensable complement. His own example at last won the students over. And it was best

[10] Dietrich Bonhoeffer, *Life Together*, SCM Press 1954; reset 1965, p. 38. All following references are to this impression.
[11] Dietrich Bonhoeffer, *The Way to Freedom*, Collins 1966, p. 35.
[12] *Life Together*, p. 87. [13] *The Way to Freedom*, p. 31.

explained by a paper written by Eberhard Bethge with Bonhoeffer's approval.

> Why do I meditate? Because I am a Christian and because therefore every day is a day lost for me in which I have not penetrated more deeply into the knowledge of the Word of God in Holy Scripture . . . Because I need a firm discipline of prayer. We are fond of praying as our fancy takes us. That is wilfulness. Prayer is the day's first service to God. God claims our time for this service . . . Meet him first in the day, before you meet other people . . . The word of Scripture should never stop sounding in your ears and working in you all the day long, just like the words of someone you love.[14]

The closing of the seminary was a great blow to Bonhoeffer. He had had there doubts and times of depression. But he could write of it to his students as 'the busiest time of my whole life, both personally and professionally' and 'I have learned more than ever before by living and working with you.'[15] He had learned much about the life of prayer and it had marked another stage for him on that road.

The police restricted his movements and watched him closely. But he managed to go to London again and then to the States, where his American friends wanted him to settle down. He soon realized his mistake. As the danger of war loomed larger and larger, he returned home. He wrote to an American friend: 'I will have no right to participate in the reconstruction of Christian life in Germany after the war if I do not share in this time with my people.'[16] On 27 July he was back in Berlin. On 1 September German troops invaded Poland. Life became more and more difficult until, surprisingly, he was taken on as an unpaid assistant to *Abwehr*, the army's counter-espionage department. In this way he knew of – and was almost certainly implicated in – all the resistance movement against Hitler. So it could not have surprised him when on 5 April 1943 his rooms were searched and he himself was driven off to the Tegel military prison in Berlin.

The first twelve days he was in harsh, solitary confinement, but he was after that treated rather better than the average run

[14] Ibid., pp. 57 ff.   [15] Ibid., p. 259.   [16] Bethge, op. cit., p. 559.

of prisoners – his uncle, General von Hase, was the city commandant of Berlin. On the day the prison gates clanged behind him, his family announced that he had been recently engaged to Maria von Wedemeyer, a nineteen-year-old girl of great beauty and character, from one of the landowning families not far from Finkenwalde. Even in his imprisonment she deeply influenced him. A fellow-prisoner remembered how 'with shining eyes he told me of the letters from his fiancée and his parents, whose love he felt near him even in prison'.[17]

To read his *Letters and Papers from Prison* and watch the unfolding of his character and of his prayer is in itself a moving experience. In the initial shock he may have been tempted to suicide. Perhaps he feared that under torture he might disclose others' names. From a cryptic note it seems he considered it, but he drew the line, he ruled it out. 'Suicide, not because of consciousness of guilt but because basically I am already dead, draw a line.'[18] He regained his equilibrium. His years of disciplined prayer were bearing their fruit in an inner freedom. He wrote, *'Only through discipline may a man learn to be free.'*[19] Even within his prison walls he found himself free to work, to serve, to pray. He rose early each morning and settled himself down to his planned days of reading and writing. He could even say, 'Unfortunately I never get through quite as much as I set out to do during the day.' He made friends with the warders. He was a steadying influence in the prison during the air raids. All his years of preparation enabled him to remain courageous and genial; and he was proud of it. Yet in his prison poem, *Who am I?*, he acknowledged that there was another side.

> Who am I? They often tell me
> I would step from my cell's confinement
> calmly, cheerfully, firmly,
> like a squire from his country-house . . .

[17] Article by Fabian von Schlabrendorff in *I Knew Dietrich Bonhoeffer*, p. 229.

[18] *Letters and Papers from Prison*, p. 35 – for comment see Bethge, op cit., p. 736.

[19] *Letters and Papers from Prison*, p. 371 (my italics).

Am I then really all that which other men tell of?
Or am I only what I know of myself,
restless and longing and sick, like a bird in a cage . . .[20]

Through it all he maintained the rhythm of his life of prayer. 'At 6.00 a.m. I like to read psalms and hymns, think of you all, and know you are thinking of me.' 'I am reading the Bible straight through from cover to cover, and have just got as far as Job, which I am particularly fond of. I read the Psalms every day, as I have done for years; I know them and love them more than any other book.' This no doubt helped him in preserving his outward equanimity and in dealing with his inner fears. He significantly closed his first page of notes with the words 'Overcoming in *prayer*'.

Yet it is rather a surprise to find him writing, 'It's remarkable how little I miss going to church. I wonder why?' – and even more surprising, 'Once again I'm having weeks when I don't read the Bible much; I never know quite what to do about it. I have no feeling of obligation about it . . . Of course, there's always the danger of laziness, but it would be wrong to be anxious about it; we can depend upon it that after the compass has wobbled a little, it will point in the right direction again.'[21]

His character was obviously maturing; but his inherited disdain for weak characters is still there. When a former Nazi district-leader, who had fallen out of favour, collapsed and was terrified at air raid warnings, Bonhoeffer said, 'I laughed outright and told him off'; and when the same man made a disparaging remark about the Jews, Bonhoeffer went so far as to say, 'I've also arranged for him to be deprived promptly of all little comforts.'

Bonhoeffer himself had to undergo nerve-racking, gruelling examination about his past contact with the anti-Hitler resistance. Then for months his case was put off and put off. After a year in prison he saw it was no good pinning his hope on an early release; he wrote to Bethge, 'If I were to end my life here', and to his parents, 'I've got used to things'.

[20] *Letters and Papers from Prison*, pp. 347 f.   [21] Ibid., p. 234.

It was the moment of *letting go*. We can date it. He had been in prison a year. He let go his hope of release. He let go as well both his attachment to a particular theological language and also his personal disdain for weaker and less gifted people outside his own circle. He was now open to be changed and ready to be surprised. So there came a breakthrough in his thinking. It has kept theologians busy ever since. And at the same time came the other breakthrough both in his relationship with others and also in his confidence in God.

Dietrich realized that again something was happening inside him, for he wrote to Bethge: 'You would be surprised, and perhaps even worried, by my theological thoughts and the conclusions that they lead to . . . What is bothering me incessantly is the question what Christianity really is, or indeed what Christ really is, *for us* today.' [22] Bonhoeffer's faith in God and in Christ never shows any sign of wavering. For him Jesus Christ is always 'the same yesterday, today and for ever', but our perception of him may change with our growing knowledge of the universe. Bonhoeffer's own knowledge had been growing. After almost despising natural science ever since he was at home with his brothers, he had now had his eyes opened by reading Weizsäcker's book, *The World-View of Physics*. He had also had this whole year in the Tegel prison, surrounded by men who were rough, half-educated, worldly, with hardly a thought beyond this world. In a strange way a 'Christian instinct' often drew him 'more to religionless people than to the religious'. He came to regard them as the typical men of the years to come. (Perhaps the present interest in oriental religions and in non-cerebral forms of Christianity indicates that the man of the future is not going to be quite so worldly or secular as Bonhoeffer expected.) He foresaw a 'religionless Christianity'. But he did not mean what we mean by religion. For Bonhoeffer 'religion' is a derogatory word. In his sense religion is just an element in the culture of the German pre-war 'establishment'. It is also, as Luther and

[22] *Letters and Papers from Prison*, p. 279 (my italics). (On the ambiguous meaning of 'us', see James Mark, 'Bonhoeffer Reconsidered', *Theology*, November 1973, p. 592.)

Barth said, our own efforts to get ourselves on the right side of God. It is using the name of God to fill up the gaps in out knowledge of the universe. And it is fleeing from our responsibilities in the world into an individualistic piety. Yet Bonhoeffer is utterly convinced that even in a 'religionless' Christianity we have to pray to God and to worship God – this we must do, but in what ways it is for us to explore.

Twice in these letters he mentions *Arkandisziplin*, the hidden discipline.[23] This means not speaking the Christian language where it might repel rather than help. It also means persevering in the hidden discipline of prayer and of Christian discipleship. Bonhoeffer would never compromise on faith. Rather, he says, the biblical faith is to be reborn in 'a new language, perhaps quite non-religious, but liberating and redeeming'. But 'our being Christians today will be limited to two things: prayer and righteous action among men. All Christian thinking, speaking and organizing must be born anew out of this prayer and action.'[24]

He knew that he was only opening doors and not yet finding solutions – that is for *us* to do each in our own situation. 'I'm only gradually working my way to the non-religious interpretation of biblical concepts,' he wrote towards the end of his prison letters; 'the job is too big for me to finish just yet', and 'it is *only in the spirit of prayer* that any such work can be begun and carried through'.[25]

This effort of radical thinking appears to have refined as by fire Bonhoeffer himself. His disdain for the weak is being burned out of him. He discovered – and perhaps this is a gentle epitaph on his dealings with that ex-Nazi prisoner whom he used to despise – that 'It is weakness rather than wickedness that drags most people down, and *it needs profound sympathy to put up with that.*'[26] And almost his last letter from the Tegel prison shows that he has come to an even more profound trust in God and prayer. The failure of the plot of

[23] Ibid., pp. 281, 286.
[24] Ibid., p. 300.
[25] Ibid., pp. 359, 379 (my italics).
[26] Ibid., p. 384 (my italics)

21 July against Hitler's life with the consequent rounding-up of all suspects had set for him the final danger signals. Now he writes that the key to everything is 'in Christ'.

> All that we may rightly expect from God, and ask him for, is to be found in Jesus Christ . . . we must persevere in quiet meditation on the life, sayings, deeds, sufferings, and death of Jesus . . . no earthly power can touch us without his will, and danger and distress can only drive us closer to him.

> Please don't ever get anxious or worried about me, but don't forget to pray for me – I'm sure you don't! I am so sure of God's guiding hand that I hope I shall always be kept in that certainty. You must never doubt that I'm travelling with gratitude and cheerfulness along the road where I'm being led.[27]

On 8 October he was transferred to the cellars of the far more formidable Gestapo prison in Prinz Albrecht Strasse. No more friendly warders to smuggle letters in and out. Neither his parents nor Maria saw him again. Only two letters survive, short and closely censored, to his father and mother. Berlin was near the breaking point. In the prison was chaos and near panic. A fellow-prisoner wrote: 'Bonhoeffer was different; just quite calm and normal, seemingly perfectly at his ease. His soul really shone in the dark desperation of our prison.'[28] The divine love had through prayer done its work in him.

The Gestapo prison was burned out in a raid on Berlin. Dietrich and other prisoners were driven south to concentration camps along the now narrow strip of German land between the American and Russian armies. He was hanged at Flossenbürg in the grey dawn of 9 April 1945. A sceptical English officer was among his companions at the end and he said of him: 'He was one of the very few men I have ever met to whom his God was real and ever close to him.'[29]

[27] *Letters and Papers from Prison*, pp. 391, 393.
[28] Letter from Captain Payne Best to Sabine Leibholz, Bonhoeffer's twin sister, quoted in Bosanquet, op. cit., p. 271.
[29] Bosanquet., op. cit., p. 272.

5

Teilhard de Chardin – Interpreter

The leaves of autumn were falling rather dismally from the tall trees in a graveyard on the banks of the Hudson river. Near it, the great house was no longer the noviciate of the Jesuits. It had been sold and of all things turned into the Culinary Institute of North America – to train not priests but chefs.

Among the rows of identical gravestones of forgotten Jesuits I found the one inscribed

Pierre Teilhard de Chardin
Born 1 May 1881
Died 10 April 1955

I stood still. I remembered him, a professional scientist, a speculative thinker, a man of deep prayer – but, above all, an interpreter. He had been called, so he was convinced, to interpret to the *modern*, scientific world, what it has *always* taken to make a Christian.

He had lived under a ban. His critics had turned him out of his beloved France. He had died suddenly from a heart attack at teatime in a friend's apartment in New York on Easter day. A mere handful of people had been at his funeral.

Yet since his death his books have sold by their hundreds of thousands. His most important work, *The Phenomenon of Man*, has a preface in its English version by Julian Huxley and in its Russian version by Roger Garaudy. It has triggered off Marxist–Christian dialogues. Scientists also and theologians are still arguing over his theses.

You would hardly expect this kind of a man to come from a family of eleven children at the Château of Sarcenat in the

Auvergne, some sixty miles from Le Puy, where Simone Weil was later to teach. His father was tall and impressive, with twirled moustache, a gentleman-farmer and an antiquarian. English periodicals – *The Field* among them – lay on his library table. He spoke little, but always to the point. His study on the first floor of a rambling house was indeed a *sanctum* – none entered unless invited. Pierre's mother used to walk two miles across the fields and back every day to early mass. She implanted in him a strong, traditional faith. This 'nugget of pure gold which was the piety and faith of his childhood' Teilhard retained to the end, as one of his later critics, Étienne Gilson, observed.[1] He owed to his mother, he said, so much – *le meilleur de moi-même*, the best part of himself. The whole household always gathered together for evening prayers in the dining-room. The family entertained a good deal but almost entirely their innumerable cousins and their families. It was a devout, closed society.

There were already signs of Pierre's remarkable future. He treasured bits of rock and especially bits of iron – a plough-spanner or steel splinters from a firing range. 'You should have seen me,' he wrote later on, 'as in profound secrecy and silence I withdrew into the contemplation of my God of iron.'[2] He was sent to a Jesuit boarding school. By chance one of his masters was Henri Bremond, the friend of Baron von Hügel and Father Tyrrell, and he noted that Pierre was 'very intelligent, and first in every subject' but 'transposing his mind far away from us was a jealous and absorbing passion – rocks'.[3]

At eighteen he entered the Jesuit noviciate. His traditional religious convictions were deepened. In fact once, after reading *The Imitation of Christ* by Thomas à Kempis, he even thought of giving up his interest in rocks for what he called 'supernatural activities'. But his common-sense novice-master

---

[1] Robert Speaight, *Teilhard de Chardin*, Collins 1967, p. 326.
[2] Pierre Teilhard de Chardin, *Le Milieu Divin*, Collins 1960; Fontana 1964, p. 18. All following references are to the Fontana edition.
[3] Cited in C. Cuénot, *Teilhard de Chardin – a biographical study*, Burns & Oates 1965, p. 4.

replied that 'his crucified Lord looked for a natural development of his being as well as his sanctification':[4] advice Teilhard never forgot.

In 1902 an anti-clerical government expelled the religious
orders from France. This Jesuit community went off incognito
to Jersey in borrowed civilian clothes. Teilhard laughed to the
end of his life about this comic episode – solemn Jesuit
Fathers in top-hats, bowlers and the primitive motoring caps
of those days. After his noviciate he was sent for three years to
teach physics in a Jesuit college in Cairo. Like others he began
to feel the lure of the East; but he was then more interested in
things than in people. He came to England to a Jesuit house at
Hastings to finish the last four years of his studies.

All this time he had been living in another closed society –
this one all-male, Jesuit-dominated, reacting against French
anti-clericalism, suspicious of anything which smelt of any kind
of modernism. Traditional faith was part of him. But he was
about to be plunged into the modern world. Brought up on the
old view of creation, he now read Bergson's *Creative Evolution*.
The liberating word 'evolution' would continue to ring in his
ears 'like a refrain, a taste, a promise and an appeal'.[5] It would
be the dominant factor in all his thinking – and in all his
praying.

Then he first world war broke out. Teilhard, now thirty-
three, was called up and became a stretcher-bearer with a
crack Moroccan regiment. He was in the front line through
most of the great battles. This intellectual, 'sheltered' Jesuit
won the Médaille Militaire and was made Chevalier of the
Légion d'Honneur. He called the war his 'baptism into
reality'. 'Fundamentally,' he wrote, 'I'm glad to have been at

[4] Ibid., p. 7.
[5] Pierre Teilhard de Chardin, *Le Coeur de la Matière*, p. 9 (available
in roneoed form from Teilhard Centre for the Future of Man, 3
Cromwell Place, London SW7 2JE; compare 'In spite of his love of
nature and his study of fossil-life, he was apparently unaware of the
controversies over Darwin, or indeed of the whole subject of evolution
until he was close on thirty' – C. E. Raven, *Teilhard de Chardin,
Scientist and Seer*, Collins 1962, p. 33.

Ypres. I hope to emerge more of a man and more of a priest.'[6]
In fact, *something new was released within him*. Later he
described these years as 'his intellectual honeymoon'. Reflections – seminal reflections – poured off his pen. He filled notebook after notebook in his neat handwriting – I cannot think
how – in the blood and mire of dug-outs. In a real sense *all*
that came later was the working out of insights received in the
trenches.

Also during the war his genius for friendship developed. He
discovered how close he was to his cousin, Marguerite. His
stream of letters to her from the front makes this clear. 'Our
friendship is precious,' he told her, and compared it to 'a note
of music, which gives tone to our whole life.' For Teilhard,
man's speculation had to be balanced by woman's intuition. He
tried not entirely successfully to work this out in his forecast
of future human evolution; but he found a clue. Towards the
end of his life he could write, 'Nothing developed in me which
was not under a woman's gaze or a woman's influence.'[7] All
this was within his loyalty to his calling. 'Love is a three term
function,' he maintained, 'man, woman and God. Its whole
perfection and success are bound up with the harmonious
balance of these three elements.'[8]

After the war he went to Paris to study geology seriously. He
received his doctorate in 1922 and then a professorial chair at
the Institut Catholique. The next year he was invited to go to
China for field-work. On the voyage out he caught sight of
Mount Sinai and wrote to his cousin Marguerite this revealing
passage:

> I should have loved to visit those rocky slopes, not only to test
> them with my hammer, but also to listen and see if I could hear the
> voice from the 'burning bush'. But has not the time passed when God
> speaks in the desert . . . for the summits where he dwells are not
> in inaccessible mountains, but in a profounder sphere of things.

[6] Pierre Teilhard de Chardin, *The Making of a Mind: Letters from
a Soldier-Priest 1914–1919* (written to his cousin Marguerite Teillard-
Chambon), Collins 1965, pp. 26, 56.

[7] *Le Coeur de la Matière*, p. 33.

[8] Pierre Teilhard de Chardin, *Human Energy*, Collins 1969, p. 76.

The secret of the world is wherever we can see the universe as something transparent.[9]

Letters from a Traveller had begun – perhaps our best introduction to Teilhard. Paris always drew him like a magnet. Letters kept him in touch. After eighteen months he was back again. Besides his scientific work, he used to try to help students in their intellectual difficulties.

Trouble started. He wrote a private, speculative paper on original sin in the light of evolution. This paper somehow got to Rome. Some think it was stolen from his desk. Pressure was at once put by Rome on the Jesuit superiors that he should be moved from Paris and should publish nothing but strictly scientific papers. Perhaps these superiors wanted to save Teilhard from more severe censures as well as to preserve their order's good name for orthodoxy. Teilhard wrote to a Jesuit friend: 'Please help me, I've put a good face on it outwardly, but within it is something resembling an agony or a storm . . . But if my ideas seem innovations, they nevertheless make me as faithful as anyone to the old attitude.'[10] Loyal he remained, faithful to God, meticulous in his prayers, his breviary, his mass and his annual Ignatian retreats.

His next departure for the East was a kind of exile just when his influence was beginning to tell in France. On the voyage he again wrote to Marguerite: 'I have certainly grown older in the last three years – even in the last eighteen months. Ideas no longer bubble up inside me with the same exuberance.' And he added, 'My vision is more direct, my grip firmer, but I feel less.'[11]

Back in the 'brooding old China' he took part in the discovery of the skull of Sinanthropus – the so-called 'Pekin man' – an important link in the chain of human evolution. And it was now that he had time to write *Le Milieu Divin*, which he

[9] Pierre Teilhard de Chardin, *Letters from a Traveller*, Collins 1962; Fontana 1967, p. 28. All following references are to the Fontana edition.

[10] Letter to Père Valesin SJ, quoted in Pierre Teilhard de Chardin, *Letters to Léontine Zanta*, Collins 1969, p. 30.

[11] *Letters from a Traveller*, p. 80.

described as 'an essay on the interior life'. But for years he was immersed in his scientific work, deep in China and in other countries. From his letters we can enjoy the perception, the courage and the humour of this inveterate traveller. Once he longed for a primitive train in Abyssinia to break down so that he could get out and take rock samples – and it did. 'For pity's sake,' begged his companion when they at last set off again, 'no more miracles.'

Often travelling by mule for days on end, he could not say mass but prayed for those dear to him and for the peoples who surrounded him.

> Since once again, Lord – though this time not in the forests of the Aisne but in the steppes of Asia – I have neither bread, nor wine nor altar . . . I, your priest, will make the whole earth my altar and on it will offer you all the labours and sufferings of the world . . . One by one, Lord, I see and I love all those whom you have given me to sustain and charm my life . . . I call before me the whole vast anonymous army of living humanity.[12]

Again we see his tall figure, wrapped in a fur wind-jacket, with a shy smile on his long, forceful face that looks as though carved out of mahogany. He gulps down boiling soup from a mess-tin as he stands in the freezing cold of the Gobi desert winter at minus thirty-three degrees centigrade.

For the whole of the second world war there was no more field-work. He was interned at Peking, so it was there that he wrote his key work, *The Phenomenon of Man*. It was written a page or two each day, synthesis of twenty-five years' thought. The ground of the book – if I may dare to try to summarize it – is the belief in the spiritual future of the earth. Man is not complete. He must become conscious of a greater cosmic process of which he is the most responsible part. The world is still unfolding in the direction of ever greater order and consciousness. We must strive in the direction of this great unifying thrust. All matter can give way to Spirit, by our knowledge and right use of it. The medium is love and faith. Under their influence the world yields and grows warm. The vehicle

[12] Pierre Teilhard de Chardin, *Hymn of the Universe*, Collins 1965; Fontana, 1970, p. 19.

(Teilhard spent more and more time on the implications of this thought) is the Christian church reborn, bearing humanity *onwards* towards a great universal centre, a supreme centre of love and personality, which is Christ.[13]

As soon as the war was over Teilhard managed to sail back to France. A great welcome awaited him. But heavier disappointments were in store. His Jesuit superiors vetoed his candidature for the professorship of palaeontology at the Collège de France. He went to Rome himself with revised typescripts of *The Phenomenon of Man*, *Le Milieu Divin* and other works to ask for an imprimatur. On his return he said to a friend at the Gare de Lyon, 'It's "No" to everything.' So once again he left Paris. His last years were at the Wenner-Gren Foundation in New York – but virtually another exile.

Perhaps the best way to understand Teilhard de Chardin and his life of prayer is to turn to his small practical book, *Le Milieu Divin*. It is translated into English; only its title is untranslatable. Here is his interpretation of the Christian life of prayer put into modern idiom. 'Rooted in the Real', we might describe it. We may have to be careful not to let ourselves be put off by his forms of expression – what another Jesuit has called 'Gallic waffle' – nor by the fact that the author is not an exact theologian nor a biblical scholar.

It is a personal book. 'It is precisely me,' he wrote to Marguerite, 'what I have been living and preaching so long.' He hoped that it 'might open new frontiers for many minds' and that it might win 'some sort of approval from the Church'. It did the first, but tragically not the second. He added: 'I want to write it slowly, quietly – living it and meditating on it like a prayer.'[14] It is a book to come back to again and again.

Significantly it is dedicated to 'those who love the world'.

[13] A beginner's introduction to this work is J. V. Kopp, *Teilhard de Chardin Explained*, Mercier Press, Cork 1964, and there is a useful glossary of his terms in Vernon Sproxton, *Teilhard de Chardin*, SCM Press 1971, p. 123.

[14] *Letters from a Traveller*, p. 91.

Many Christians at that time – a higher proportion than now – took a jaundiced view of this world. They had been taught that the more they separated themselves from the world, the nearer they would come to God.[15] From that view Teilhard saw two evils might follow. First, many Christians might live narrow, impoverished lives – and the more vast the universe was discovered to be, the more fearful and withdrawn they would become. Secondly, this narrowness might repel further from the church many modern people, whose outlook is being shaped by evolution and modern science; they already have 'the suspicion that our religion makes its followers inhuman'. Teilhard is aiming to show how 'the love of God and the healthy love of the world' should nourish one another.

So next he shows how *all our actions*, secular as well as religious, can be divinized or, as we might say, consecrated – and this, because according to the New Testament we can 'put on Christ' and so live our whole lives in union with him. This we can do by uniting our intention in every task to the divine will – as tradition has always taught – but Teilhard went a step further and said that every work of ours could have value in itself and become a part of God's great reintegration of all things in Christ (Eph. 1.10). This can give us *élan*, 'a certain passionate delight in the work to be done':

> He awaits us every instant in our action, in the work of the moment. There is a sense in which he is at the tip of my pen, my spade, my brush, my needle – of my heart and of my thought.[16]

But in order to be able to live and work in this way we need those 'cherished moments' when we give ourselves to prayer and receive the sacraments, 'for without these times we should soon forget this ever-present tide of the divine omnipresence'.

[15] Confusion has arisen because Christians have not distinguished clearly enough that the Bible uses the same word 'world' in two senses: (i) the whole created reality and the world of peoples created by God (Ps. 90.2; John 3.16; Acts 17.24), which is how Teilhard understands it; (ii) humanity in rebellion against God (James 4.4; I John 5.19), which is how men use it who decry the world. See J. J. von Allmen, *Vocabulary of the Bible*, Lutterworth Press 1968, pp. 469–70.

[16] *Le Milieu Divin*, p. 64.

These times set apart for prayer are not to be – as they have been sometimes in the past – regarded as 'a burden of observances and obligations to weigh us down and increase the already heavy load'; but rather they can in fact become a spring 'of immense power which bestows significance and beauty and a new lightness on what we are already doing.' So many of the men and women in this book have discovered for themselves this power of prayer.

To work in this spirit can itself unite us to God by detaching us from our lower selves. For work of this kind implies 'effort and a victory over inertia'. We experience 'the painful pangs of birth' in creative action. We jettison outworn ways of expression as we 'go in search of new forms'. We 'spread' our 'sails and are borne by a current towards the open seas'. It is through all these actions that 'the Christian knows that his function is to divinize the world in Jesus Christ'.

Then Teilhard de Chardin goes on to show that it is also through the hardships we endure that the world is divinized. Teilhard underlined in writing what he had himself experienced in life. He is no arm-chair adviser. He speaks of injustices that come to us from others, of fears that well up from within us, of accidents and illnesses. We have to learn, he says, how to cope with these; and, even if we seem to be getting off more lightly than other people, we know we all have to face the inevitability of our own death.

Yet among Christians there is sometimes a false resignation to suffering. This makes us feeble in spirit and gives unbelievers something to scoff at. Teilhard regarded this cowardly resignation as a bigger obstacle to the conversion of the world than scientific and philosophical objections. We must first fight these evils – 'as long as resistance is possible, the son of heaven will resist'. Only afterwards should there be resignation – and then positive resignation.

Sometimes we may have to fall like 'soldiers during the assault which leads to peace'. And often we can see our sufferings as the Lord's pruning knife among the vines, which is going to lead in the end to better fruit. We have to be ready even to tear up our own roots on our journey to God. And always we must realize that for those who love God 'all things are working together for good' (Rom. 8.28). Very touchingly he writes a prayer:

> When the signs of age begin to mark my body (and still more when they touch my mind) . . . in all those dark moments, O God, grant that I may understand that it is you . . . Teach me to treat my death as an act of communion.[17]

Always in the Christian life there is this rhythmic alternation of actions to do and hardships to cope with – attachment and detachment. Detachment is no good for detachment's sake, but only for further growth. So the Cross remains fundamental to the Christian life. It is the essential place of renunciation. But it is also the beacon to direct us along a sacrificial road which expresses love – a road steeply climbing upwards. 'The Christian is not asked to swoon in the shadow but to climb in the light of the Cross.' Never in the steepness of this climb must we fall into the crude error of thinking that spirit and matter stand in opposition to one another like good and evil. On the contrary matter, the tangible setting of our lives, is holy matter and it gives us footholds in our ascent.

But we are not climbing to a remote God. He is here. He touches us within, especially through our fellow men and women.

> By means of all created things, without exception, the divine touches us, penetrates us and moulds us . . . It nevertheless possesses in a supreme degree that precise concentrated particularity which makes up so much of the warm charm of human persons.[18]

Of all this we are confident because of the incarnation of Christ; it is this that discloses the divine love: 'the human-divine contact was revealed at the epiphany of Jesus'.

There is no pantheism here, though some of Teilhard's phrases in isolation might look like it. 'Our divine *milieu* is at the antipodes of false pantheism.' Teilhard remains a Catholic and in a sense a traditional Catholic at heart, though with a universal outreach. We come to God, he reminds us, not as mere individuals, but as the church, the mystical body of

[17] Ibid., pp. 89–90.
[18] Ibid., pp. 112–13.

56

Christ, with her sacraments. 'We rejoin the great highway opened up in the church by the onrush of the worship of the holy eucharist.' He means not only the sacrament at the altar, but also 'the sacramental species formed by the totality of the world', and sees 'the duration of the creation as the time needed for its consecration'. We remember the 'Mass of the world' in the woods of the Aisne and the steppes of the Gobi desert. And so he resolves to react to the eucharistic contact 'with the entire effort of my life . . . and of my life as linked to all other lives'.

All this finds its focus for him in profound and passionate adoration of God, which Teilhard believes is a fundamental need of man fully awakened to reality.

> What I cry out for, like every being, with my whole life and all my earthly passion, is something very different from an equal to cherish; it is for a God to adore.
> The more man becomes man, the more will he become a prey to a need, a need that is always more explicit, more subtle and more magnificent, the need to adore.[19]

The width of Teilhard's sympathies and the profundity of his mysticism never remove him from the basic simplicities of Christian faith. He, the scientist, calls us to believe firmly that prayer has a real, tangible effect. But it must be the prayer of faith: 'Ask, and it will be given you.' It may not normally change events outwardly (though miraculous effects *may* follow), but it invests them with a new spiritual power, recasting them, transforming them on a new, higher level. He is also firmly convinced of the reality of heaven – and of hell; though he prays that no one will be lost and adds in parenthesis: 'and I know, my God, that you will forgive this bold prayer'. He affirms that all salvation is through Christ who, in a certain sense, will be the only one saved, and others saved through him and in him – 'Christ the head and living summary of humanity'. So in heaven we shall contemplate God through the eyes of Christ. And Teilhard follows the gospel in looking forward to the *parousia*, the unpredictable second coming of Christ, and he affirms, 'We have to *expect* it.'

[19] Ibid., pp. 127–8.

Teilhard, the prophet of the 'real', calls Christians at the end of this now famous little book to be 'as passionately vowed to spreading the hopes of the Incarnation', as others are to building up their Utopian cities. How can such a Christian impetus come? Teilhard prays: 'Jesus, compel us to discard our pettiness and to venture forth, resting upon you, into the uncharted ocean of love.'

Yet all through his writings and letters you feel the man is even greater than his message.

He is first gripped and held by his calling to identify himself with the questioning, scientific minds of his time in order to interpret for them the agelong 'unsearchable riches of Christ'. He is one with his great Jesuit predecessors of the seventeenth century; di Nobili, identifying himself with the Hindu scholars of Madurai, and Ricci with the mandarins of China.

Secondly, through his sufferings his own humanity was deepened and enriched. This was the making of him. This is why, as a fellow Jesuit scientist in China wrote:

> The look in his eyes when they met your eyes revealed the man's soul; his reassuring sympathy restored your confidence in yourself. Just to speak to him made you feel better; you knew he was listening to you and he understood you. His own faith was in the invincible power of love.[20]

Thirdly, his keyword is fidelity – fidelity through sunshine and cloud, in the life of prayer and in the life of service. 'Through fidelity and fidelity alone can we return to God the kiss he is for ever offering us across the world.'[21]

[20] Ibid., Introduction, p. 13.
[21] Ibid., p. 138.

6

Dag Hammarskjöld and Alan Paton – in World Politics

Towards the end of *Le Milieu Divin* Teilhard de Chardin remarked that humanity is still imprisoned in its narrow loyalties. Then he went on to prophesy – and we may see this before the end of this twentieth century –

> A tremendous spiritual power is slumbering in the depths of our multitude, which will manifest itself only when we have learned to break down the barriers of our egoisms and, by a fundamental recasting of our outlook, raise ourselves up to the habitual and *practical vision of universal realities*.[1]

If we wish to be men and women of prayer, we have the responsibility of keeping our eyes open to the ends of the earth and of being alert to realities of practical politics. We saw how Isaiah, a man of prayer, was concerned with social justice; he was equally concerned with the blessing of peace – peace between the warring great powers of his day, Egypt and Assyria, and peace for the small Jewish people caught up between them: 'The Lord of hosts will bless them: a blessing be upon Egypt my people, upon Assyria the work of my hands, and upon Israel my possession' (Isa. 19.25).

In few places do you realize the need for a just peace more than in Africa. I felt it when I stood near Ndola in Zambia, where Dag Hammarskjöld was killed, and also in Durban, where I talked with Alan Paton in his home. Both men have played their part in world politics. Prayer has been central to their lives. Both – and this may be an encouragement to

[1] Pierre Teilhard de Chardin, *Le Milieu Divin*, Fontana 1964, p. 146 (my italics).

us – have come to real prayer through great difficulties, in lives packed with work and responsibilities.

It was towards midnight on 17 September 1961 that Dag Hammarskjöld, the Secretary-General of the United Nations, was killed in a plane crash near Ndola – whether by sabotage or accident we shall probably never know – on a journey to try to end the war in the Congo.

After his death the manuscript of *Markings* was found beside his bed in his apartment on East 73rd Street in New York. They are jottings of a spiritual diary kept for over thirty-one years, written for no eyes but his own. They were published; they came as an enormous surprise. Nearly everyone had taken this international diplomat, this reserved man, who very seldom went to church and who drove himself hard with a will of steel, to be an agnostic humanist dedicated to the service of mankind. As a matter of fact he had modestly stated his fundamental faith in a short broadcast when he first came to New York eight years before. But this had been forgotten. The book sold like wildfire but, as an American bishop remarked, 'Everybody owns Dag Hammarskjöld's *Markings*. Few have read it. Few of these have understood it.' I must say, when I first read it, I couldn't make much of it, except towards the end. It seemed a jumble. It came to life for me when I read it again alongside Henry van Dusen's book, *Dag Hammarskjöld: a Biographical Interpretation*, which skilfully places these jottings in the context of Dag Hammarskjöld's life. I would advise you to have these two books side by side.

He was born in the same year as Madeleine Delbrêl, 1905. His family lived in the splendour of a sixteenth-century castle at Uppsala, a university city. I once made a pilgrimage there to his grave near to the cathedral. His ancestors on his father's side had been chiefly soldiers and politicians; and on his mother's, clergymen and scholars. His mother had a deep influence on him. He was brought up as a rather liberal Lutheran. At the university his faith was eroded. This kind of scepticism is no modern thing. It has been with us for generations now. In the eighteenth century David Hume, the sceptical philosopher, said: 'Of course I never criticize religion in front of the servants.' The difference now is that there are no servants and scepticism has a good press!

Dag Hammarskjöld did very well as a student. He also became a connoisseur of art and a keen mountaineer. Soon after leaving university he went into finance and government service. His future looked 'made'. Then he was elected Secretary-General of the United Nations. The challenge of this key post was for him 'the greatest of blessings as well as the greatest of burdens'.[2] For eight years he lived a well-packed life – working at his always tidy desk with seldom more than a couple of papers on it, making difficult decisions, facing tough men like Kruschev, travelling the world. 'He was a man of quiet but incredible energy,' a colleague said, 'I have never worked with anyone who seemed so impervious to fatigue.'[3] People often say to us: 'If you live at this kind of pressure, it will steam-roller your religion out of you. But with Dag Hammarskjöld it was precisely the opposite. It was then that his life of prayer really grew. But it had been a hard road.

I have now read *Markings* several times. Of the many things that strike me, perhaps I may highlight four.

First, the way to faith – or the way back to faith – is, for him and for many like him, often a long journey. For months nothing new or illuminating turns up. I know this road myself. We feel inclined to give up the search. But then there come 'moments' – moments of disclosure. We examine them carefully. We don't want to be taken in. But these correspond, we find, to what other searchers claim to have found. And these illuminate other experiences, sometimes what we might call 'secular' experience. They help us to look at our own lives in greater depth. These 'moments' are sometimes clear and memorable, like Simone Weil's; but by no means always.

On this particular point Dag Hammarskjöld's development is especially interesting. Clearly he had a 'moment', but he didn't know when he had had it. Only retrospectively could

[2] B. Urquhart, *Hammarskjöld*, Bodley Head 1973, p. 23.
[3] Ibid., p. 29.

he realize what a breakthrough it had been; it may be so with some of us. He writes about this in a passage that is, to me, moving and clearly authentic (and remember the kind of man he was, with an analytical, critical mind):

> I don't know Who – or what – put the question. I don't know when it was put. I don't even remember answering. But at some moment I did answer *Yes* to Someone – or Something – and from that hour I was certain that existence is meaningful and that therefore my life in self-surrender had a goal.[4]

I quite realize that different people come to God in different ways, or, rather, that God finds us in different ways. But those lines are really worth pausing over. That one passage would make the book for me.

Secondly, he examined and reflected on the writings of those who claimed to have some kind of *first-hand experience* of God. Some of these men and women were the mystics. What is significant about the mystics, all are agreed, is not the strange and unusual experiences they may have had, but that this contact which they claim to have with God through prayer brings a wider and deeper love into their lives. I do not think that Dag Hammarskjöld was a systematic student of the mystics. But he quoted St John of the Cross in that first broadcast in New York. There are also passages of Eckhart in *Markings* and Thomas à Kempis from 1953 onwards. He spoke to a friend about the medieval mystics just as he was boarding the plane for his final journey and said: 'Love, for them, was a surplus of power which they felt completely filled them when they began to live in self-forgetfulness.'[5]

Dag Hammarskjöld also reflected on the experience of Jesus Christ. Some people today come to their knowledge of Jesus Christ through reading the mystics first, and it may have been so with Dag Hammarskjöld. Why not, even if it is not very logical? It was doubtless Christ's sense of intimate fellowship with God – call it, if you like, mystical – which gave the Lord himself 'the

---

[4] Dag Hammarskjöld, *Markings*, Faber 1964; paperback ed. 1966, p. 169.
[5] H. P. van Dusen, *Dag Hammarskjöld: a Biographical Interpretation*, Faber 1967, p. 219.

driving force and source of energy for an almost impossible mission'. This heroic dedication to his mission, even to death, is what seems most to have attracted Dag Hammarskjöld to Jesus Christ.

It was their experience of God which drew Dag Hammarskjöld also to the Psalmists. The later part of *Markings* is full of references to the Psalms. Almost his last entry, apart from three very characteristic poems, was words from Psalm 78 – 'And they remembered that God was their strength.' Many people by praying the Psalms or parts of them have come to love them and know them by heart. These familiar verses have helped to maintain their faith, and indeed their sanity – Bonhoeffer's in his prison and Hammarskjöld's on his exhausting journeys.

Thirdly, he had to do some hard thinking for himself – and this may well be so for many of us if we are to have an authentic life of prayer. 'There is no formula to teach us how to arrive at maturity,' he said to some students , 'and there is no grammar for the language of the inner life.'[7] He could not take over patterns of belief from others, however intellectual or however holy they might be. He wrote about 'my never abandoned effort frankly and squarely to build up a personal belief in the light of experience'. He maintained that it was honest thinking that finally led him round to the beliefs of his youth; in the end he recognized and 'endorsed unreservedly', he said, 'those very beliefs which were once handed down to me'.[8] And, as I read his words, I cannot help thinking of those lines of T. S. Eliot, who made a similar pilgrimage from faith through agnosticism to deeper faith:

> We shall not cease from exploration.
> And the end of all our exploring
> Will be to arrive where we started
> And know the place for the first time.[9]

[6] C. H. Dodd, *The Founder of Christianity*, Collins 1971, p. 52.
[7] Urquhart, op. cit., p. 17.
[8] Broadcast talk on arriving at New York, quoted in van Dusen, op. cit., pp. 46–7.
[9] T. S. Eliot, *Little Gidding* V in *Four Quartets*, Faber 1968.

'And know the place' – although we've been there long before – 'for the first time'. That was Dag Hammarskjöld's experience too.

Fourthly, what is very striking to me in this diary is where his great steps towards faith and prayer come. 'The years of his most rapid advance in faith and prayer were', as van Dusen says, 'precisely his years at the United Nations, years packed and overflowing with the problems and intricacies of world political affairs.'[10] Could anything be more distracting, more destructive, do you think, to a quiet, steady life of faith and prayer than the intricacies, the rivalries, the hostilities, the personal tangles in which he was caught up? But that is where prayer for Hammarskjöld deepened. He wrote: 'For many of us in this era the road to holiness necessarily passes through the world of action.'[11]

On his flight from the Kennedy airport to the Congo he had with him, as always on his long journeys, a pocket edition of Thomas à Kempis' *Imitation of Christ*, and as a bookmark in it a postcard, on which was typed his oath of office as Secretary-General of the United Nations.

There are a few books – once you have read them, you live with them. Alan Paton's first novel, *Cry, the Beloved Country*, is one of those books for me. It brings back to me again and again the 'feel' of the green rolling hills and villages in Natal and of Soweto, the enormous African location outside Johannesburg. It makes me care. The injustice on one side and the resentment on the other between the races is world politics. What happens in any country affects the others.

When Dag Hammarskjöld's plane crashed in Zambia, Alan Paton was just at the mid-point of his fifteen years' service to the Liberal Party in South Africa, which welcomed equally Whites, Blacks, Coloureds and the Natal Indians to its membership. Indeed Alan Paton has given his life to fighting for a multi-racial society in South Africa. And he acknowledges that it is through prayer that he has received strength and courage for this task.

[10] van Dusen, op. cit. [11] *Markings*, p. 108.

64

On a recent visit to South Africa I spent a long afternoon with him in his bungalow surrounded by a profusion of flowers looking down the Valley of a Thousand Hills towards the Indian Ocean near Durban. I should think he is about seventy. He has a care-lined face, with a shock of untidy white hair; he looked like a rather tired, angry old lion. We talked about how things were developing in South Africa, and I could not help recollecting that disturbing sentence of his novel: 'I have only one great fear that one day when the Whites are turned to loving, they will find us, Blacks, turned to hating.'[12] Then he told me how he came to give his life to this multi-racial cause.

He was born in Pietermaritzburg in Natal. His parents were Christadelphians, anti-Catholic, anti-Anglican, anti almost everything and very puritan. He reacted against this, as many of us would have done. He became an unbeliever, a determinist. He read maths and physics, took an educational diploma and started teaching at a high school in the little town of Ixopo in Natal. There on a tennis-court he fell in love with a flirtatious young wife, six years older than himself. Defying her family, she had married a man with advanced tuberculosis, and it was not long before he died. After a suitable interval Alan and this young widow married. He tells the story of his first marriage in a very delicate way in his book, *Kontakion For You Departed*.

When they were married they went back to Pietermaritzburg, where he taught. Then at thirty-two he was put in charge of the Diepkloof reformatory for seven hundred delinquent Africans, just outside Johannesburg. He stayed thirteen years – and transformed it from an insanitary, appalling kind of prison into a school with a large degree of freedom. He had compassion and courage. Every time he made a change the staff threw up their hands in horror. There were moments when anything might have happened and this extraordinary experiment might have collapsed. But it came off.

[12] Alan Paton, *Cry, the Beloved Country*, Jonathan Cape 1948; Penguin 1958.

Interested now in the whole question of prisons, he set out in 1946 on a tour of Europe and North America to study penal reform. And it was at Trondheim in Norway, when he had visited the cathedral and marvelled at the evening light through a lovely rose window, that he went back to his hotel and wrote that haunting sentence which opens *Cry, the Beloved Country*: 'There is a lovely road that runs from Ixopo into the hills.' He wrote out of homesickness, he told me. He was homesick for his wife and for his country, and the novel, he said, just came off his pen like this; it was like opening up a new vein of gold. And as he travelled, he kept writing. He started it in Norway in September and by February, in San Francisco, he had finished it. On his return the first thing he did was to put it into his wife's hands.

His health was not good; he took it easily for a time, yet presently he became the national chairman of the Liberal Party. He told me he was taken aback by the hatred which this drew upon him; he said, 'I couldn't believe it.' The same hatred – and also fear – was behind much of the repressive legislation by the Nationalists in South Africa.

After his wife's death he married a second time; and a divorced woman. This caused some trouble with the Anglican church in South Africa. But that has been resolved. He has recently written the life of Geoffrey Clayton, one of the wisest and most courageous archbishops of Cape Town.

As I talked with Alan Paton, I sensed that he was a man of prayer. He has not written much on it. *Meditations for a Young Boy being Confirmed* was in fact for one of his sons. He wrote it, he told me, in a cabin among those immense redwoods just outside San Francisco. He also had published some reflections on the prayer of St Francis of Assisi, *Instrument of Thy Peace*. Malcolm Muggeridge has put them in the same class as Simone Weil's *Waiting on God* and Dietrich Bonhoeffer's *Letters and Papers from Prison*; that I think is pitching them a little too high. But they are very moving, specially if you can feel your way into the situation in which they were written. He was by the bedside of his wife in her two years' illness, an almost continuous struggle to breathe. It was in the extreme tension just after Sharpeville, where sixty-seven Africans were shot down by the police. He and his wife had to sit by and see the police search their personal papers. He was given the tip that he was to be arrested, but at the last minute nothing happened.

But the significant thing about these reflections on prayer is that they come from the pen of an *ordinary* man. Most of the people we are meeting in this book are such extraordinary people – Charles de Foucauld, so hard on himself; Bonhoeffer, so courageous; even Madeleine Delbrêl, nearer to ourselves, so competent – that they both encourage – and discourage – us. 'What's the good of us trying?' we say. Then comes Alan Paton with faults like most of us.

He becomes irritated with what seems to him a needless accumulation of doctrines and with the *laissez-faire* attitude of the church. The failure of his high hopes of political change and the long illness of the wife he so loved bring on the most fundamental doubts. We want to believe, he says, but can't. Depression sometimes settles down on us too. There is no hope, no faith, no one to pray to. There is bleak despair; we continue to breathe, to eat and to drink, but there is nothing more we can do. Fortunate we are, if some friend understands and comes to draw us out of ourselves, as Clare, at the risk of some scandal, once visited St Francis, for even he had his hours of despair. If by temperament we are anxious, we may have to accept our anxiety like a physical disability – and just get on as best we can. There are times when we are paralysed by fear. And fear can't be got rid of just by our own effort, but only by finding ourselves caught up into a cause greater than our own interests. Alan Paton writes: 'I give my own testimony that when I am tempted to despair . . . I pray or speak or read this prayer of St Francis – "Lord, make me to do some work of peace for thee" – and *I am moved to act on it*.'[13]

He told me in conversation: 'Whatever the mood, I just have to go on, my prayer morning and evening and also

[13] Alan Paton, *Instrument of Thy Peace*, Fontana 1969, p. 44 (his italics).

67

praying before every decision.' He said about the companionship of fellow-Christians and about holy communion – 'Without those I couldn't go on.' Here has been his strength in struggles for justice and humanity. In his confirmation meditations for his son, he prayed these two lines to our Lord in holy communion:

> I said in my heart to him, I who in sins and doubts and in my grievous separation reach out my hands,
> Reach out thy hand and touch me, O most holy One.[14]

[14] Alan Paton, *Meditations for a Young Boy being Confirmed*, SPCK 1959, section xi.

68

7

Thomas Merton – Contemplative

A solitary Trappist monk in heavy boots with a wind-jacket over his white habit looks out from the edge of the forest towards the haze of the hills of Kentucky. This is Thomas Merton. Almost all his adult life had been spent within the high walls of the silent, austere, abbey of Gethsemani in the valley beneath him. The last three years he had with the consent of his abbot lived in an even deeper silence and solitude in a hermitage hidden among the woods on the monastic lands.

Yet when he died on 10 December 1968, people all over the world – Christians, people of other faiths and non-believers – felt the shock of losing someone they loved. Why was this? They would answer, 'He understood me.' This feeling came across not only in conversations and letters, but in his books as well, for as someone said, 'His writing was himself.' And people would add, 'He gave me just the word of encouragement that I needed.' That 'word' Thomas Merton would, I think, have summed up as – 'Contemplation can open in your heart a spring of love and joy in the world as well as in the cloister.'

He understood others through what he had gone through himself.

He was born during the first word war in the French Pyrenees of a New Zealand father and an American mother, both artists, with typically artistic temperaments. His mother died from cancer when he was a boy of six and his father was always on the move. So Tom had a mixed up education, in the States, in France and in England. At Cambridge he did the first part of a Modern Languages course – and then departed rather under a cloud. He had never been happy there. He returned to the States and finished his studies at Columbia, New York with a thesis on 'Nature and Art in William Blake'. He did some journalism and wrote poetry. He had left-wing sympathies and visited Cuba. His life was fairly permissive, and he had had no serious contact with Christian belief until an Indian guru – of all people – recommended him to read the *Confessions* of St Augustine and *The Imitation of Christ* by Thomas à Kempis.

He began to dabble in religion. One weekend he put off a girlfriend and on Sunday morning went for the first time in his life to mass. It was at Corpus Christi church just off Broadway. He sensed what worship was; and as he listened to the priest speaking about God's love coming to us in Jesus Christ, something woke up inside him. It was the moment of his conversion. As he came out of church into the sunshine of Broadway, he said: 'All I know is that I walked into a new world.'[1] It is like falling in love. Colours are brighter. Our sensitivity is heightened. But like love conversion is not emotion only; it moves on to reflection and commitment. He asked for instruction. In baptism he committed his life to God, and searched how best to serve him. First he tried teaching in a Franciscan school, but they told him he had no vocation there. Then he went for Holy Week to the severe Trappist monastery of Gethsemani. At once he felt that this was the place for him, and it was.

He now said he did not wish to see his name in print again – this ambitious young writer. For he believed that if he could have this desire for fame, this egoism, purged out of his life, he could be linked more closely to the reality of God. Then his life and his prayer would together become a channel for God's love. And this, he was convinced, would be the best service he could give to the world.

Life in the monastery was tough. He became an exemplary novice and a true monk. His abbot asked him to write the

[1] Thomas Merton, *Elected Silence*, Hollis & Carter 1949, p. 167.

story of how he 'came to the light'. This turned out to be a very long book, *The Seven-Storey Mountain*. A slightly abbreviated version, *Elected Silence*, came out a little later in this country. I remember reading it when it first appeared. I couldn't put it down. You felt Tom Merton was with you talking to you, you shared his feelings. But I slightly disliked the man. He was too religious, too earnest, a bit too narrow for me. Whether I liked him or not, the world liked his book and it became the third best-seller in the world. He must, as a young Trappist monk, have felt bewildered and embarrassed. Anyway, his abbot told him to go on writing. He became a prolific writer. He wrote too much. He was a man of enthusiasms; a close friend called him *überschwenglich*, exuberant.

He produced a charming book, *The Seeds of Contemplation*, though apart from one reference to Karl Marx and one to the first atomic bomb, it might have come out of any good medieval cloister in Europe. Then ten years later he wrote another, *The New Seeds of Contemplation*. When you put these two books side by side, you notice that something extraordinary has come to Thomas Merton. You can turn it up in his diary, *Conjectures of a Guilty Bystander*, and see what it was. One day he had to go into the neighbouring town to see a doctor. It is a lovely drive through beautiful country, where they distil gin and train race-horses. There, in the town with hundreds of Americans milling around, it happened.

> In Louisville, at the corner of Fourth Avenue and Walnut Street, in the centre of the shopping district, I was suddenly overwhelmed with the realization that I loved all these people, that they were mine and I theirs . . . It was like waking from a dream of separateness . . . This sense of liberation from an illusory difference was such a relief and joy to me that I almost laughed out loud . . . To think that such a commonplace realization should suddenly seem like news that one holds the winning ticket in a cosmic sweepstake.[2]

This I would call his 'second conversion'. In Corpus Christi church, Broadway, he had been converted to God transcendent, God the Lord of all. In the shopping district of

[2] Thomas Merton, *Conjectures of a Guilty Bystander*, Burns & Oates 1968, pp. 140-1.

Louisville he was converted to the world, or rather to God immanent in his world and in his people. But far from becoming a worldly man in the pejorative sense, he became a finer monk. This experience gave richness and breadth to his already profound life of prayer. From this all sorts of things fanned out.

He persuaded his abbot to widen the outlook of the community. They managed to invite fundamentalist Southern Baptists to the monastery guest-house – and this, long before John XXIII made ecumenism fashionable. Thomas Merton advocated nuclear pacifism in the coldest days of the cold war. He pleaded for disengagement from Vietnam long before American students were marching and protesting. He sensed the coming of Black Power, and already in 1963 he wrote *Letters to a White Liberal* to wake others up. He was in touch with *avant-garde* poets in South America, corresponding with them in Portuguese and Spanish. Of course it wasn't all plain sailing; he had to put up with much misunderstanding.

And he began to be interested in oriental mysticism. He had no intention, as he was sometimes accused, of making a mish-mash of Christian and oriental beliefs, but rather of exploring all their underlying contemplative experiences. He was concerned to share 'not only information about doctrines' which he explicitly declared 'are totally and irrevocably divergent; but also religious intuitions and truths which may turn out to have something in common, beneath surface differences'.[3] His hope was, as he later expressed it, that 'by openness to Buddhism, to Hinduism, and to these great Asian traditions, we stand a wonderful chance of learning more about the potentiality of our own traditions.'[4] The book he said he most enjoyed writing – and he put into it five years of hard work and meditation – was *The Way of Chuang Tzu*,[5] a Taoist philoso-

---

[3] Thomas Merton, 'Contemplation and the Dialogue between Religions', *Sobornost*, Series 5, No. 8, Winter–Spring 1969, p. 563.

[4] *The Asian Journal of Thomas Merton*, SPCK 1944, p. xxiv.

[5] Thomas Merton, *The Way of Chuang Tzu*, New Directions, NY 1965, p. 9.

pher of the third century BC. Thomas Merton even began to learn Chinese.

One thing always amazes me about Merton and other men of prayer – how they find the time. He spent hours in liturgical prayer, in personal prayer, in daily routine work; and yet he had time for all these other things. It is true that people who knew Merton say that he never wasted a moment; he had things organized in that sense. Yet it is quite fantastic. I can only guess that when one really loves God, there is a kind of inner explosion of insight and energy. It may then be that the Holy Spirit sets things off and releases what is there already, as in a sort of way human love sometimes does. We saw a similar thing in Charles de Foucauld's hermitage at Tamanrasset.

The wider and greater his interests, the more Merton felt drawn to a deeper life of prayer. After ten arduous years as novice-master, he was after much pleading with his abbot allowed to live alone in a hermitage in the woods that he loved near the monastery. He wrote to a friend: 'I know, if one can ever be said to know, that this comes from God and that I must obey him.' I have myself visited his hermitage. It is simply built of light prefabricated blocks on a cement floor. There is, besides a small sleeping-room, one fair-sized, all-purpose room, with a fireplace, a solid working-table, and a large window right along one side, looking on to a verandah. Electricity and running water were added later on and also a little chapel. He cut his own wood, made his fire, cooked his own food. He rose each morning at 3.00 a.m. for prayer. In his diaries he speaks with great happiness of those silent hours before dawn.

His whole life took on more and more a contemplative tone. This came out, for example, in the way he used a camera, which he received from a friend on a protracted loan. He photographed leaves piled up haphazardly against a tree trunk, the grain in the wood of a felled tree, the wind-raised ripples in the snow, even paint-spattered cans. He didn't arrange things, he let them speak to him as they were. He used his lenses as contemplative instruments. Just so, his friends on their rare visits to his hermitage found themselves welcomed receptively. As Dietrich Bonhoeffer had discovered when he was growing in prayer, the world is 'looking for an ear that will listen'. Thomas Merton had come to find this as the *raison d'être*, the essence of his life as a contemplative: 'In reality the monk abandons the world only in order to listen more intently to the deepest and most neglected voices that proceed from its inner depths.'[6]

Yet finally a dream of his life came true, a visit to the Orient. He had seldom left Gethsemani. Now his abbot sanctioned this long trip. 'It all just dropped out of the sky,' Tom wrote to a close friend. 'Naturally I have done my pushing, too. Once it all began. But I had no inkling that it would ever begin.' He flew from San Francisco to Bangkok; he wrote in his diary: 'The moment of take-off was ecstatic. The dewy wing was suddenly covered with rivers of cold sweat running backward. The window wept jazzed shining courses of tears. Joy. We left the ground – I with Christian mantras and a great sense of destiny, of being at last on my true way after years of waiting and wondering.'[7] In the East he had long conversations with the Dalai Lama and Tibetan monks; he stayed with Hindu monks and, in Ceylon, with more Buddhist monks. He was open, receptive, all the time learning. In his notes for a great conference in Calcutta of men of many faiths, he wrote:

I have left my monastery to come here not just as a research scholar or even as an author (which I also happen to be). I come as a pilgrim who is anxious to obtain not just information, not just 'facts' about other monastic traditions, but to drink from ancient sources of monastic vision and experience.[8]

Rumours went round the world that he had given up being a Trappist, even that he had left the church. But in fact he continued to say mass; and although he had his abbot's permission to look for another and a more remote hermitage, he

[6] Thomas Merton, *Contemplative Prayer*, Darton, Longman & Todd 1973, p. 25. First published as *The Climate of Monastic Prayer* Irish University Press 1969.
[7] *The Asian Journal*, p. 4.
[8] Ibid., pp. 312–13.

said in the last letter he wrote: 'With Christmas approaching I feel homesick for Gethsemani. Best love to all.'

He returned to Bangkok for a strategic conference of oriental abbots. While there he showed the manuscript of his most important book, the quintessence of his teaching, to a friend of mine, Dom Jean Leclercq, a Benedictine from Luxembourg. It is a book, I think, for all of us to read. It has been published as *Contemplative Prayer*, with a discerning preface by Dr Douglas Steere, a Quaker.

One morning at this conference Thomas Merton read a radically exciting paper on 'Marxism and Monastic Perspectives'.[9] It makes clear that his absorption in contemplation and indeed in Buddhist and Hindu mysticism had not diminished his concern with the world of politics. He quoted Marcuse and international, neo-Marxist student leaders, whom he had met at Santa Barbara before he crossed the Pacific, as well as quoting Teilhard de Chardin. He maintained that the monk, as much as these revolutionary students, 'is essentially someone who takes up a critical attitude towards the world and its structures'. Thomas Merton was clearly far from having solved his problems; he has left us plenty to do. But what a lively discussion everyone expected when the conference resumed later that day. After lunch Tom went for his siesta. When he did not reappear, they looked for him. They found him dead through an accident with an electric fan. He was only fifty-three. His body was flown back to Gethsemani. At his requiem there the abbot said: 'Father Louis' (as he was called inside the community) 'was a young brother, he was a very young brother, and had he lived to be a hundred he would still have been a very young brother' – because he was a man whose eyes and ears were always open, he was always listening to what was coming from the hearts of men and women the world over, and searching for light in that deeper intimacy with God through prayer and contemplation.

'I believe that the capacity of the ordinary Christian for contemplation,' Archbishop Michael Ramsey has said, 'is

[9] Ibid., pp. 326–43.

greater by far than some of our theories of the spiritual life have allowed.'[10] Neither the Archbishop nor I are using this word in a narrowly technical sense. Contemplating, like loving, is of many kinds; and, like love, it is by no means emotional only; and ultimately they are both 'too deep for words'.

Not always does contemplation seem to be a directly religious experience. You can certainly begin long before all your religious problems are solved. I would like to share with you an experience of mine in the mountains. Many years ago – but I have never forgotten it – I did a stiff climb up to a high col. It was quite an effort to make the last few feet – and suddenly before me was a circle of towering snow-capped peaks glittering in the sunshine. First, I was speechless, taken out of myself; time stopped. Next, I drank in, I received into myself some of the grandeur and beauty. Then, something was waking up inside me, I was responding, and a new sensitivity was being given me. In the end, as I began to go down, the effect lasted; I recognized a new beauty around me and particularly in the weathered faces of peasants in the village below. Through all this I had received a sense of unhurriedness, of beauty, of human appreciation leading nearer to love.

Never was contemplative experience more needed than today. Many of us are living in a world that is all out for efficiency and speed. It is pressurizing us, hurrying us into treating men and women as 'types' rather than as persons, because we haven't, we think, time – or love – for more. So we need this experience frequently – if possible, daily – to keep us warm and human, just as friends and lovers feel the need to meet or at least to write frequently. We can't leave this to chance; we must plan. Love is in us, but it wants to be expressed, renewed and deepened.

Each of us has then to discover how to create for ourselves opportunities for contemplation. Our 'hermitage' may be a back room. We may look at a bowl of flowers on the table, or at a tree through the window. We may go out for a walk in

[10] A. M. Ramsey, *Canterbury Essays and Addresses*, SPCK 1964, p. 29.

streets or fields, daytime or night, and experience, like Words-
worth, 'a sense sublime of something far more deeply inter-
fused'; or more profoundly some may with the intuition of
Christian faith be able to say, like the twentieth-century mystic
Joseph Mary Plunkett,

> I saw His blood upon the rose
> And in the stars the glory of His eyes.

Simply look at a crucifix, an icon, a work of art or the holy
sacrament in church – and something of the divine love may
come through to you. It can happen through music, perhaps
a particular disc, and through poetry, secular or religious. I
remember the day when the lines –

> My song is love unknown,
> My Saviour's love to me,
> Love to the loveless shown,
> That they might lovely be –

suddenly became for me no longer lines, but something rich,
multi-dimensional. Sometimes, often, it is memories that set
us off. We may remember how God, how Christ, became
real for us at some unforgettable time, perhaps at holy communion. What was real then remains in a deep sense real now,
even if indistinct; and we can journey on in the strength of the
spiritual meat and drink then given us. Some of us too can
feed contemplatively on experiences of human friendship and
love, genuinely sacramental of the divine love. There are
many other ways. Personally I start usually from some
treasured passage of the Bible, because for me the Bible is,
like our Lord himself, really human with the divine shining
through. I have met him there before, and he will meet me
there again. I read a few verses each evening and let them
simmer in my mind. The next day he is there for me in quiet
contemplative prayer. I often can't feel his presence, but deep
down I know.

Whatever our way, we have to learn how. And it means
going steadily on through every kind of mood and weather.
But I have found more spring days than I expected. Basically

for me it is like my mountain experience. First, I need some way of quietly focusing my attention, of not feeling hurried, even if time is rather short. A short time with a friend is far better than no meeting at all. Secondly, I've had to discover how to be receptive. When the son comes back from the far country, the father is there first, he's down the road to meet him. To be receptive to that welcome and love is the *heart* of prayer. Thirdly, I want to respond, as you do because we are human, to respond as deeply as we can – though we can't always feel it very deeply. We do our best, and God by his Spirit within us will help us to respond. Finally, we shall all find, if we go on trying, that this will gradually change us from inside. 'He who loves God, loves his brother' (1 John 4.21). To become contemplative is to become human, to learn to love truly. We have watched this happening in Thomas Merton.

But we have seen that it means a long exploration, evoked by love and sustained by love. Yet Thomas Merton makes it clear that we experience genuine contemplation, as we experience true love, '*only* as a gift, and not as a result of our own clever use of spiritual techniques'.[11] We have to learn how to be open, how to desire, how to wait expectantly.

Neither contemplation, nor loving, is smooth going. 'Contemplation', Thomas Merton used to say, 'is no pain-killer.' We may find, for example, that our old simple concepts of God dissolve, and we seem lost in a Godless darkness. We may have, as Thomas Merton knew well, 'to face the terrible experience of being apparently without faith *in order really to grow in faith*.'[12]

However difficult it may be to go on through this blankness, which sometimes seems like spiritual *ennui*, we know this is the road other explorers have trod before us. We must not be engrossed in our own inner difficulties. We must keep our eyes open to the needs of the world around us; we cannot go wrong in that. For 'no man who ignores the rights and needs of others can hope to walk in the light of contemplation, because his

[11] *Contemplative Prayer*, p. 115 (his italics).
[12] Ibid., p. 97 (my italics).

78

way has turned aside from truth, from compassion, and therefore from God'.[13]

The secret of Thomas Merton's understanding and love for all kinds of people and his concern for justice and fraternity in the world were nourished and illuminated by his silent, demanding hours of prayer and contemplation. So, I am becoming convinced, it will be with us and with the renewed church.

> Without contemplation and interior prayer the Church cannot fulfill her mission to transform and save mankind. Without contemplation she will be reduced to being the servant of cynical and worldly powers, no matter how hard her faithful may protest that they are fighting for the Kingdom of God.[14]

[13] *New Seeds of Contemplation*, p. 15.
[14] *Contemplative Prayer*, p. 144.

8

Michel Quoist – Sociologist and Priest

Christians of the traditional type are – to put it mildly – seldom fond of most sociologists who talk about religion. In fact I remember an ecumenical conference in the autumn of 1972 of the leaders of the churches in Great Britain held at Birmingham, and how Cardinal Heenan told us there that sociologists were his *bêtes noires*.

Michel Quoist is a sociologist, a man of the people and a Roman Catholic priest. He is a man of today; he thinks, he writes, he prays from *within* our present situation. He makes this clear at the beginning of *The Christian Response*, which of all his books speaks most clearly to me personally and is the most probing. He writes first of 'the awesome problem of social injustice' and of 'the untold suffering everywhere visible in the world'. He knows South America well. But then he goes on to analyse 'another cancerous disease, more menacing still because it is even more devastating . . . the interior disintegration of man himself'.[1] This, it seems to me, is what lies behind the demand for a 'counter-culture' by students in so many nations, and not only by students. But Quoist will have no *simpliste* solution. No Gandhi's spinning wheels for him. He will have no truck with trying to reverse the technological revolution of the last thirty years. He will go through it and beyond it. 'Today we find ourselves confronted with the gigantic task of undoing or rather of re-doing what has already been done . . . We have to remake man so that the

[1] Michel Quoist, *The Christian Response*, Gill & Macmillan 1965, p. vii.

universe may be remade through him, in conformity with a pattern of order and love.'[2] What is needed is the exploration of what love is and demands; and in this exploration Quoist believes prayer is an essential part.

Le Havre is his home. He was born there in 1921. He had to start work at fourteen, as his father died very young. He was influenced by the Jocists – *Jeunesse Ouvrière Chrétienne* – a Catholic youth movement. It had begun just before the 1914–18 war. Joseph Cardijn, a Belgian boy, from a working-class home like Michel Quoist, had started his training for the priesthood. His father, a small coal merchant, had continued to work after he ought to have retired, in order to support his son. The father died, Joseph came home to the funeral from the seminary. He knelt beside his father's body and vowed to give his life to spread the faith among young workers and to secure for them fairer working conditions. I was in close contact with cells of this movement before and after the 1939–45 war, and helped to start similar groups – the short-lived Christian Workers' Union – in industrial parishes of the Anglican church.

At eighteen Michel Quoist was able to enter the seminary, but he kept in touch with the Jocists. After his ordination in 1947 he was sent to Paris and took a doctorate in social and political studies. He is no remote, arm-chair sociologist. During part of this period of study he shared the life of some of the lowest-paid workers. The first book he had published was a sociological study, *The City and Man*. He then worked as assistant priest in a large, proletarian parish in Le Havre. Soon he was appointed chaplain to the youth groups of the region. Then the French bishops made him secretary of their project *Fidei Donum* to help Latin America. This involved much travelling. But now he has been relieved of these responsibilities and has returned to be the parish priest of an important church in Le Havre.

He does not claim to be a professional writer. He still

[2] Ibid., pp. viii, x.

travels a good deal. He scribbles down notes on a pad in a plane or metro or train. He files them systematically. When the moment to write comes, he sits down and puts them into shape. He passes them on to others for their frank comments. Then he gives them their final form.

He is also much in demand as a speaker. A few years ago he spoke to a large congregation in the university church at Oxford; he gripped our attention, even though speaking through an interpreter. We were impressed by his sincerity, his practicality and his realism; it is to *our* situation that he speaks.

The obvious way for you to meet Michel Quoist is to read and re-read his *Prayers of Life*.[3] It has sold over two million copies in two dozen languages. His other books help you to understand his approach. The book *Prayers of Life* isn't everyone's cup of tea. I don't think it's mine. Why will become clear as I write. But the more I read it, the more I learn. Each of us has to discover his own way of prayer, but people very different from ourselves may give us clues. And Michel Quoist is far better than some of his imitators.

These *Prayers of Life* ring true. They are not 'composed' prayers, as Michel Quoist explained in a letter to me. They emerged from actual groups of Christians in concrete situations. They are 'the daily life of committed Christians offered to God' – '*Elles sont la vie de militantes et de militants offerte à Dieu, jour après jour.*'[4] So these prayers, naturally colloquial – even more so in the French – strip away the formalism, sentimentality and Pharisaism of much conventional praying. Some of them may shock – like the one about a pornographic magazine – and shock to good purpose. They have galvanized into prayer again many people who had become bored and tired with their own superficial prayers and routine churchgoing. These prayers are not intended, of course, as Quoist says, to replace the liturgy and the prayers of the church. Their great value is to show people that it is

[3] Michel Quoist, *Prayers of Life*, Gill & Macmillan 1963; translated from *Prières*, Editions Ouvrières, Paris 1954.
[4] *Prières* (original French), p. 11.

the ordinary events of daily life that they should reflect on and pray about in their own genuine, spontaneous words. So it is better – in my opinion – *not* to pray the prayers of Quoist, but to let these prayers set you free to pray in your own words, where you are, with a genuineness and spontaneity as real as his. He himself actually gives this advice in *Meet Christ and Live:* 'This book should be read – and then forgotten.'[5]

Yet we shall each find some memorable phrases which lodge in our minds and remain with us as catalysts for our own praying and living. I shall not forget the words about Mary, the Lord's mother: 'She walks in the crowd, unknown, but she doesn't take her eyes off you.'[6] Sometimes whole passages have a haunting beauty. In *Prayers of Life* there is a word-picture of the sea, all the more striking because as we should expect most of his images come from the city.

To find time to pray is *the* problem for many of us today – and time to care for other people. I know this well myself. We saw how Madeleine Delbrêl found her own answer. Quoist has wrestled with this problem in his life, too. Read the meditation called 'Lord, I have time' in *Prayers of Life* to discover his answer.

Quoist warns us not to take on things rashly in a moment of enthusiasm. Look at the day before it begins, he says. See that there's time for prayer, as there's time for meals. Concentrate on the one thing before you – the letter, the conversation, or whatever it is. To do two things at the same time – or to half do each of them – is what wears you out. Let an interruption quite replace what you are doing, but then go straight back to what you were doing. Never say you are overwhelmed with work, or you will soon believe it. When you feel you are reaching your limit, stop, breathe, pray. That is an economy of time – and a renewing of your strength. At the end of the day, place your work through prayer in God's hands and *leave* it there.

[5] Michel Quoist, *Meet Christ and Live!*, Gill & Macmillan 1973, p. 12.
[6] *Prayers of Life*, p. 121.

We all know the times when everyone wants us at the same moment. Michel Quoist prepares us to meet these occasions.

> While men came in to you,
> I, your Father,
> I, your God,
> Slipped in among them.[7]

It takes a long time, he reminds us, to learn how to care truly for others.

> Believe me, it's a long apprenticeship, learning to love,
> And there are not several kinds of love;
> Loving is always leaving oneself to go to others.[8]

Nor are we to be discouraged when we fail. The Lord says:

> Ask my pardon
> And get up quickly.
> You see, it's not falling that is the worst,
> But staying on the ground.[9]

Our basic difficulty is committing ourselves and the future to God; we are afraid to do that.

> But I am afraid to say 'yes,' Lord.
> I am afraid of putting my hand in yours, for you to hold on to it.[10]

Michel Quoist is not a systematizer. He gives us guide-lines, clear guide-lines, but encourages us to find our own way. In summarizing his advice, I will try not to make it more precise than it is.

'Dialogue with Christ' is his favourite description of prayer. 'The important fact is that we are invited to meet Jesus, to talk with him, to love him, so that we may be transformed and united in a common undertaking.'[11] Christ is the way the Father comes to us and the way we go to the Father. God comes to us and speaks to us through Christ in the gospels, but also through the events of life – 'that new gospel to which we ourselves add a page each day'.[12] God often speaks to us

[7] Ibid., p. 92.
[8] Ibid., pp. 39 f.
[9] Ibid., p. 106.
[10] Ibid., p. 94.
[11] Michel Quoist, *Christ is Alive!*, Gill & Macmillan 1971, p. 120.
[12] *Prayers of Life*, p. 2.

through young protesters, even when they are unfair and violent, because 'they shake us out of our habitual complacency and our self-satisfaction with a way of thinking and a life-style which we no longer question sufficiently'.[13]

Like the Jocists, he lays stress on the scriptures, specially the gospels: 'You can receive these words of life over and over again; their depths are unfathomable . . . But you can't encounter the Lord and hope to understand his word unless you've first asked the Father to be your guide and the Spirit to be your interpreter.'[14] Quoist can't understand a Christian not turning expectantly to the New Testament. 'Would you let your fiancée's letter lie unopened on your desk? Why then do you let the gospels stand unopened on your bookshelves?'[15]

He expects Christians, including young industrial workers, to aim at some kind of praying, however brief, at the beginning and end of the day, and during it. He must have realized how much he was asking of them, because he had lived in their homes and shared their lives. But he is a realist; he knows that unless we pray regularly, we shan't stay the pace.

Each morning he recommends us to glance at the gospel and to have at least a short time for prayer. This then will help us during the day to maintain our contact and dialogue with Christ. 'When you are upset, busy or tense, take a moment to renew your offering of love and you will then find yourself working more effectively.'[16] Here, Michel Quoist has translated for us what Père de Caussade, a perceptive guide of the seventeenth century, in his *Self-Abandonment to Divine Providence* inspiringly called 'the sacrament of the present moment'. Because the very nature of God is love, de Caussade taught, God radiates his love incessantly to us. So God desires to transmit to us his love not only in the holy sacrament, but in and through *every* happening of our lives. Therefore we should try to train ourselves – it is the task of a lifetime – to

[13] *Meet Christ and Live!*, p. 7.
[14] *The Christian Response*, p. 161.
[15] Ibid., p. 161.
[16] Ibid., p. 82.

approach each event, each personal contact, expectantly, receptively, just as we approach the sacrament. Teilhard de Chardin did it – and had this openness and serenity. To the man of our time, so conscious of all the pressures upon him, Michel Quoist says: 'God is waiting for you here at this very moment, at this very place *and nowhere else.*'[17]

At the end of the day be recommends a quiet review of what we have done – in the light of what God says to us through the gospels and through the circumstances of our lives. And this review, he says, 'should lead spontaneously to prayer: a four-dimensional prayer of praise, thanksgiving, penance and petition'.[18] And Quoist the sociologist is insistent that our prayer should be no individualistic pietism; rather it ought to be concerned with society and with changing its structures. There are many meditations, especially in *Meet Christ and Live!*, which illustrate this.

To give time regularly to God is, Michel Quoist reiterates, vital. It is an indispensable sign of our love for God, just as a husband not only works for his wife, but also gives her time day by day.

> Don't say: I haven't time to pray, but that doesn't make any difference, I offer my work up and that's a prayer. Love demands that you stop for a while. If you love, you must find the time to love. To pray means to stop for a while; it means to give some of your time to God, each day, each week.[19]

Nor, without regular praying, shall we see and serve the Lord in the circumstances of our life, 'for in order to see him and understand what he says, you have to look for him and listen to him in those brief daily encounters which prayer makes possible'.[20] Nor again must prayer depend on our fluctuating feelings.

> You will never attain to a life of authentic prayer so long as you are looking for an emotional experience . . . On your part, the value of your prayer depends upon the effort it demands of you.

[17] *The Christian Response*, p. 72 (my italics); see also p. 89.
[18] Ibid., p. 170.
[19] Ibid., p. 175.
[20] Ibid., p. 176.

86

On God's part, the value of your prayer depends upon the action of the Holy Spirit within you.[21]

Michel Quoist, like many other guides, tells us that as our prayer develops and deepens, we may need fewer words. Our prayers may become more simple, more contemplative.

> To contemplate God is to look at him and love him. This attitude, however, simple as it is, is the end result of a process. To try to attain silence too quickly is dangerous, for silence, although it can serve to convey a fullness of love which no word or gesture can contain, can also serve to interrupt a conversation.[22]

Yet, he insists, 'the silent prayer which has moved beyond words must always spring from everyday life, for everyday life is the raw material of prayer.'[23] But undoubtedly this silent prayer, like the quiet intimacy between close friends, can do much to strengthen love, which is the world's great need.

You see there is much to be learned from his books. But a few issues arise in my mind; there are indications that Michel Quoist himself is aware of them. Yet I had better mention them, but don't let these things put you off from reflecting carefully on what he has to say.

First, I myself was nearly put off by his sometimes rather 'nagging' tone. He goes on and on and on. In all fairness we should make allowance for the fact that nothing he has written, with the possible exception of *Christ is Alive!*, was written as a book. They are a collection of occasional pieces. Yet Michel Quoist – like some preachers and other people – sometimes seems to use free prayer, not so much as words addressed to God, but as sermons obliquely preached *at* us. The effect may be to induce in us an excessive — an almost pathological – sense of guilt. Monica Furlong, in her book, *Travelling In*, has reacted even more strongly against this trend in Quoist.[24] But don't let this put us off.

[21] Ibid., pp. 176–7.
[22] *Christ is Alive!*, p. 157.
[23] *Prayers of Life*, p. 22.
[24] See Monica Furlong, *Travelling In*, Hodder & Stoughton 1971, pp. 79–84.

Secondly, he appears to me to expect us to do too many things – earning our living, attending union or professional association meetings, making protests about social evils, having time always for our families and neighbours and keeping open house – with the result that we may drive ourselves to desperation, or alternatively spread our efforts too widely for them to be effective. I would like von Hügel's comment on Quoist.

Thirdly, although I am sure he would recommend the reading of good, modern commentaries, isn't Quoist – and others like him – encouraging a rather over-simple reading of the scriptures? Have not modern scientific and psychological studies so widened the distance between the first and the twentieth centuries that we cannot read off from the New Testament simple, plain answers to our contemporary problems – to cite only one instance, the position of women in the modern world? There are disclosures in scripture which we cannot treasure too highly, but must we not beware of 'a too close-sighted view' of scripture, as Dr Krister Stendahl of Harvard Divinity School, has called it? Yet I'm not sure what Charles de Foucauld would have said about this.

Fourthly, in his enthusiasm for modern scientific progress Michel Quoist seems to me to try to find a divine sanction for it by almost identifying it with the growth of the Body of Christ and with the final gathering of all things into one in Christ. We find the same thing in other modern writers, but is it legitimate?

Yet no one could accuse Michel Quoist of muffling the challenge of the Christian life. In particular he knows that progress in the life of prayer – as in love – is often hard and costly. He and his companions have known the doubt and darkness which most of us have to pass through. But they have persevered through darkness, until light dawned, and out of this experience of prayer comes their own deep love in their apostolate and daily life.

9

Anthony Bloom – the Eastern Orthodox Tradition

New York, London, Moscow, Pekin. They have met. They will meet more profoundly. The future of the church and the world depends largely on how they meet.

We need to listen to the voice of the East, to the voice of Eastern Orthodoxy. And also to voices from even further east. At the end of his life Thomas Merton was listening very intently to those further-off voices. I am beginning to realize how much I myself need to listen to *all* these Eastern voices.

I have vivid memories of a conference in Switzerland late in the fifties during the week of prayer for Christian unity. A Belgian monk spoke about Roman Catholicism, a pastor from Zürich about Protestantism; I was asked to read a paper about Anglicanism and Anthony Bloom, one about Eastern Orthodoxy. It was Father Anthony who became the pied piper of the conference. I am not quite sure why – whether it was what he said or what he was. Certainly his paper was informative and helpful. But he also charmed us all – this dignified, black-robed figure with his piercing eyes and impressive beard, speaking usually in a clear, measured French and occasionally in an English all the more attractive for its foreign accent. He told us something about his experience and this added interest to all he said.

It was in Switzerland that he had been born in 1915, the son of a diplomat of Czarist Russia. At the time of the 1917 revolution his father was serving in Persia. The family decided to cut their losses. They travelled by horse-cart and barge to the Persian Gulf and then by boat to India. They took a passage to Southampton, but the boat was too old for service. They only managed to sail to Gibraltar. They eventually settled in Paris in real poverty. From the age of twelve Anthony taught younger children for three or four hours each evening to earn his own school fees. He nearly wore himself out. He studied classics, then natural science and went on to the medical school, qualifying as a doctor just as war broke out in 1939.

But inportant things had happened to him in the meantime. At eleven he had been sent to a boys' summer camp and was impressed by a young priest there who had time and love for everyone, bad and good alike. This, Father Anthony told us, was the first deep spiritual experience he had known, but the memory of it soon to all outward appearance slipped into the background. Until he was fourteen his family had been scattered about Paris; then they managed to find a house for the first time and lived together. He had battled through hardship and brutality. But now he had happiness, yet an aimless happiness, as it seemed to him. So he resolved that, unless he found some purpose in life within a year, he would commit suicide. He had no faith. He belonged to a Russian youth group, and one evening under pressure he went in a surly mood to hear a lecture on Christ and Christianity. The rest must be told in his own words:

> I hurried home in order to check the truth of what the lecturer had been saying. I asked my mother whether she had a book of the gospels because I wanted to know whether the gospel would support the monstrous impression I had derived from this talk. I expected nothing good from my reading, so I counted the chapters of the four gospels to be sure that I read the shortest, not to waste time unnecessarily. And thus it was the gospel according to St Mark which I began to read. I do not know how to tell you what happened. I will put it quite simply and those of you who have gone through a similar experience will know what came to pass. While I was reading the beginning of St Mark's gospel, before I reached the third chapter, I was aware of a presence. I saw nothing. I heard nothing. It was no hallucination. It was a simple certainty that the Lord was standing there and that I was in the presence of him whose life I had begun to read with such revulsion and such ill-will.[1]

[1] Article by Anthony Bloom in *We Believe in God* ed. R. E. Davies, Allen & Unwin 1968, p. 26.

And that impression, he says, has never left him.

So deeply did it affect him that in time he and two companions wished to live together in a monastic community. But there was no Orthodox community in France and they had no money to found one. Yet they put in some very hard thinking. When Father Anthony was quite determined – and in spite of the age and sickness of his grandmother and mother who were dependent on him – he was allowed by his spiritual guide to take monastic vows alone privately. Then he asked, 'And who should I obey?' The reply he received was: 'It's very simple. Consider your mother as your abbot and everyone who needs you and asks anything whatever of you as your superior, and obey them unconditionally.' Father Anthony added:

> However, just then these things were made much easier. One week later I was mobilized into the French army and I had an absolutely wonderful superior – my corporal. I began to discover monastic obedience as conceived by the Desert Fathers – an absolute, unconditional obedience, going to the limits of perfect absurdity – and the wonderful sense of liberation that that sort of obedience gives.[2]

Then about his life of prayer he said:

> There was a time (during the war, and during the first five years after the war, when I was working) when I had a rule of prayer that varied between eight and five hours a day. Then at a certain moment my spiritual father forbad me to have any fixed rule of prayer and said, 'Now learn to pray unceasingly. Take liturgical prayer as your support, but don't depend on it.'[3]

He served in the army until the fall of France, then worked as a surgeon in a Paris hospital and became a member of the French resistance movement. In 1948 he was ordained priest. The next year he came to England as Orthodox chaplain to the Anglican-Orthodox fellowship of St Alban and St Sergius. He was appointed the year after as vicar of the Russian parish in London under the patriarch of Moscow. In 1958 he became bishop, in 1962 archbishop, in 1963 exarch for all the congregations in Western Europe under the Moscow patriarchate

[2] Anthony Bloom, 'My Monastic Life', *Cistercian Studies*, viii, 1973, 3, pp. 191–2.

[3] Ibid. p. 197.

and in 1966 he was raised to the rank of Metropolitan. So at least once a year he visits the patriarch of Moscow, preaches in churches there and lectures to their seminarists.

All through his experiences he has remained at heart very much a Russian Orthodox. It was this that struck us most of all at that conference in Switzerland. And for us to encounter Orthodoxy, as a Russian theologian wrote to an English friend in the last century, is like 'rushing into a new and unknown world' – a world that has known neither our Middle Ages, nor Reformation, nor Counter-Reformation, nor the Enlightenment of the eighteenth century, nor the rise of modern science, nor of modern historical research and its application to biblical study.

Personally I am sure we can gain much from reflecting on his published addresses – and that is what his books consist of with inevitably a good deal of repetitiveness. But there are questions I must put, as we should always do, even to those we most admire. There are statements which I frankly do not understand. How can Archbishop Anthony affirm that God is present in a church 'in another way than in the rest of the world'? and go on to say: 'Outside it God acts when he can and how he can; inside a church he has all power and all might.'[4] And he tells of a priest visiting a Russian church where there was a well-known, wonder-working icon and then asserts – I do not know on what grounds – that suddenly the priest 'felt that the Mother of God in the icon was as it were compelling him to pray, directing his prayers, shaping his mind'.[5] Again in a meditation on an icon, the Archbishop can write: 'Mother of God, if you withhold forgiveness, nothing can save me from damnation.'[6] He also makes statements for which I can find no evidence: for example, that Mary did not weep at the crucifixion, or that for years blind Bartimaeus had

[4] Anthony Bloom, *Living Prayer*, Darton, Longman & Todd 1966, p. 67.

[5] Ibid., p. 69.

[6] Anthony Bloom, *School for Prayer*, Darton, Longman & Todd 1970, p. 72.

sat begging at the gate of Jericho and that probably prayer and sacrifice had been offered in the temple for his healing. And there are various slips. Mother Julian is not the author of the anonymous *Cloud of Unknowing*, John Vianney was not the curé d'Ars in the eighteenth century, in fact he went there in 1818. There is no clear evidence that St Paul wrote the epistle to the Hebrews. The Greek word *eleison* for 'have mercy' does not come, as Archbishop Anthony maintains, from the same root as the Greek word *elaion* for 'oil', and so some of his ingenious exegesis in these addresses falls to the ground. But these are minor blemishes.

A greater difficulty I personally find is in the record of his televised interview with Marghanita Laski, entitled 'The Atheist and the Archbishop', which opens his book, *God and Man*. He says that for himself and for a number of other people the real life of faith began with *'an experience that was totally convincing'*.[7] I do not question that this is how it felt to him at his conversion. But this raises for me two important questions. Is it not true that for many people the life of faith comes more gradually, in the way that human friendships usually grow? So are we not putting needless obstacles in people's way if we suggest that for a living faith they *need* first of all a totally convincing experience? Secondly, although the Archbishop says that we must use reason to investigate the implications of this kind of experience, yet he does not use reason to test the validity of these experiences. Maybe some of these experiences are delusions. Just as some love affairs turn out on longer investigation to be infatuations and not love. I think he evades Marghanita Laski's probing question on this point, whether or not 'this feeling that we have encountered is something other than oneself'. In support of his position the Archbishop also quotes Hebrews 11.1 as 'faith is certainty about things invisible', but the meaning of this verse is rather: 'Faith is not in itself the proof, still less the evidence, of what

[7] Anthony Bloom, *God and Man*, Darton, Longman & Todd 1971, and Hodder & Stoughton 1974. But some people may have to start to pray without a definite belief in God; see my book, *Why Pray?*, SCM Press 1970, chapters 1–3.

is unseen. Rather it is the *mode* by which invisible realities become real to men.'[8] Whenever we are given such experiences which elicit faith, we know that they must be tested. Dag Hammarskjöld was concerned with this kind of testing. Faith, like love, eventually establishes its authenticity; as the New Testament says: 'Even gold passes through the assayer's fire, and more precious than perishable gold is faith which has stood the test' (I Peter 1.7).

Archbishop Anthony is also, I think, so exigent and stern – his own upbringing may help us to understand this – as to be in danger of discouraging some of those whom he wishes to help. He writes near the beginning of his first book about prayer:

> Unless we are ready to surrender ourselves without reservation to the divine fire and to become that burning bush of the desert, which burned but was never consumed, we shall be scorched, because the experience of prayer can only be known from the inside and is not to be dallied with.[9]

It is true that in the gospels themselves there is the note of judgment. Yet, when there is only a flickering desire, our Lord would never 'snuff out the smouldering wick' (Matt. 12.20). And in our Lord's teaching on prayer the first and predominant note is the invitation to trust in God as a merciful Father. Professor Jeremias after a minute examination of Jewish and early Christian documents has shown that when Jesus spoke to God as *Abba*, his native Aramaic word, he was speaking to God 'as a child speaks with his father, simply, intimately, securely'; and he authorizes his disciples 'to participate in his own communion with God'.[10] In a television interview Archbishop Bloom said that, compared with West Europeans, there was an element of untamed ferocity in Russians. I think in his passionate earnestness he overdoes the ferocity.

[8] H. W. Montefiore, *Epistle to the Hebrews*, A. & C. Black 1964, p. 186.

[9] *Living Prayer*, p. 10.

[10] Joachim Jeremias, *The Central Message of the New Testament*, SCM Press 1965, pp. 21, 28.

Yet, when I have said all this, I acknowledge with gratitude how much wisdom there is for us to reflect on in these addresses of Metropolitan Anthony. To any who do not know him, I would suggest that they begin with his *School for Prayer*.

Prayer is a serious matter; some of us need warning against a flabby cosiness in prayer. We remember the experience of Peter when the Lord appeared to him after a blank night of fishing.

> He realizes that he is in the presence of something, of someone, greater than he can conceive of. He is seized with a reverent awe, falls down at Jesus' feet and cries, 'Depart from me. I am a sinful man'. At that moment he has an intuition of the majesty of him who was present among them.[11]

We should preserve even in our personal prayers an element of that awe and wonder, that beauty and love that fills the liturgy of the great churches of Moscow. Though it is years and years since I was there, how vivid my memories of them are!

> It is only with a feeling of fear, of adoration, with the utmost veneration that we can approach this adventure of prayer . . .
>
> We all know what it is to love someone with all one's heart; we know the pleasure, not only of meeting, but even of thinking of the beloved, the warm comfort it gives. It is in this way that we should try to love God, and whenever his name is mentioned, it should fill our heart and soul with infinite warmth.[12]

Archbishop Anthony recommends that the very words of prayer should be chosen with care and said with deep reality.

> The first thing which I suggest, therefore, is that you should ask yourself what words of prayer make sense for you to offer to God, whether they be your own or those of other people. Ask yourself also how much they touch your heart . . . How can He receive them as an expression of love if you do not put your heart into them, if you have only put in a certain amount of courtesy together with a certain amount of absent-mindedness?[13]

We should remember that at home the Eastern Orthodox Christians use manuals of prayer, which are largely selected

[11] Anthony Bloom, *Meditations on a Theme*, A. R. Mowbray 1972, p. 36.
[12] *Living Prayer*, pp. 12–13.
[13] *School for Prayer*, p. 23.

95

from the corporate worship of the church, so that lay-people say the same prayers that are being said by the priests, the monks and the nuns in their daily office; and in these manuals the need for an inner attention is emphasized, if we are to offer '*living* prayer to the living God'. It is far better to say only a few words 'with attention and devotion, rather than to recite them all in haste and without due concentration'.[14] The mere words, Archbishop Anthony reiterates, are barren, and we need to learn

> to speak to God without breaking the silence of intimacy by words. If we can do that, we can use any form of worship. If we try to make worship itself out of the words we use, we will get desperately tired of those words, because unless they have the depth of silence they are shallow and tiresome.[15]

We find in his books plenty of advice on how to come to this silence of intimacy. An old lady once said to him soon after his ordination: 'Father, I have been praying almost unceasingly for fourteen years, and I have never had any sense of God's presence.' He replied: 'Set aside fifteen minutes a day, sit still in your room, then take your knitting and knit before the face of God. I forbid you to say a word of prayer. You just knit and enjoy the peace of your room.' What was the result? She came to Father Anthony again and said: 'When I sit quietly, face to face with him, I feel wrapped in his presence.'[16] Here may be a clue for some of us in our exploration.

This quality of silence, which is a kind of simple, contemplative prayer, can give depth and reality to all our praying, including our intercession. There must also of course be a sincerity in intercession, as Archbishop Anthony rightly insists: 'Prayer being a commitment, we cannot pray in all truth for those whom we are not ourselves prepared to help.'[17] And he goes on to quote St Isaac of Syria: 'Do not reduce your prayer to words, but rather make the totality of your life a

[14] Timothy Ware, *The Orthodox Church*, Penguin, 1963, pp. 310–12 his italics).

[15] *Living Prayer*, p. viii.

[16] *School for Prayer*, pp. 59–62; *Living Prayer*, p. 119.

[17] *Living Prayer*, p. 74.

prayer to God.' When this is becoming so, intercession and contemplative praying can come very close together. This was true of Staretz Silouan, a monk in our times on Mount Athos. He was in charge of some young Russian peasants who came to the workshops of his monastery there to earn money for their families. He used to pray particularly for a young husband, Nicholas, only twenty, who had left his wife and baby behind in his village.

> In the beginning I prayed with tears of compassion for Nicholas, for his young wife, for the little child, but as I was praying the sense of the divine presence began to grow on me and at a certain moment it grew so powerful that I lost sight of Nicholas, his wife, his child, his needs, their village, and I was drawn by the sense of the divine presence deeper and deeper until of a sudden, at the heart of this presence, I met the divine love holding Nicholas, his wife and his child, and it was with the love of God that I began to pray for them again.[18]

But this merging comes only through the discipline of the Christian life and prayer. Discipline is not something to shrink from. It means discipleship, being like the first disciples, *loving* and following the Lord. How often people, even Christians, misunderstand this.

> When we think of spiritual discipline we usually think in terms of rules of life, rules of thinking and meditation, rules of prayer, which are aimed at drilling us into what we imagine to be the pattern of the real Christian life. But when we observe people who submit themselves to that kind of strict discipline, and when we ourselves attempt this, we usually see that the results are far less than we would expect. And this generally comes from the fact that we *take the means for the end*, that we concentrate so much on the means that we never achieve the end at all.[19]

Some of us may need an experienced guide – a staretz, as the Russians would say – to help us both to discover a discipline appropriate to ourselves and also to follow it in this positive enriching way. We have noticed several times in this book how vital it is to turn to God during the course of the

[18] *School for Prayer*, p. 75.
[19] *Meditations on a Theme*, p. 14 (my italics).

day. Many of the Eastern Orthodox do this by repeating the words 'Lord Jesus Christ, Son of God, have mercy on me, a sinner' or some simple variation of this Jesus prayer. Anthony Bloom said that this came to him in his teens like 'a revelation about the life of prayer'. Some Christians in the West have also grown to know and treasure this prayer through the short Orthodox classic, *The Way of a Pilgrim*. In his preface to a recent edition of it Metropolitan Anthony has emphasized how valuable it can be to have a guide to help us in the use of this prayer as well as in our whole Christian life.

He also tells us to remember always both the good raw material that is within us and also the hands of God, who is longing to fashion us. Our discipline is a way of putting ourselves into these hands of love – and of letting us fix our eyes on that love.

> Certain things in us belong already, however incipiently, to the kingdom of God. Others are still a chaos, a desert, a wilderness . . . And we must have faith in the chaos, pregnant with beauty and harmony. We must look at ourselves as an artist looks, with vision and sobriety, at the raw material which God has put into his hands and out of which he will make a work of art, an integral part of the harmony, the beauty, the truth and life of his kingdom.[20]

All the time our eyes must be on the living God of love; and although he has disclosed himself once for all in Jesus Christ, 'the same yesterday, today and for ever', yet our apprehension of him in prayer and in life must never cease to grow.

> It is the living God, that every human soul from millennium to millennium is in search of – a God so different from the static images offered by the manifold successive religions. St Gregory of Nazianzus, in the fourth century, said that when we have gathered from the scriptures, from tradition and from the experience of the church, all that man has been able to know of God, and have constructed a coherent image from it, however beautiful the image may be, we have only constructed an idol. Because, as soon as we make an image of God and say, 'Look, this is God,' we transform the dynamic, living, unfathomable, infinitely profound God who is our God, into something limited, of human dimensions . . . All that we know of God is yesterday – it is not today or tomorrow.[21]

[20] *Meditations on a Theme*, p. 9.
[21] Ibid., pp. 70–1.

10

Frère Roger and Taizé

'For two years now I have called myself an atheist, but during this last month of my work camp at Taizé I have been to church three times a day, and as a matter of fact I'm now always looking forward to the next time of worship. How shall I ever explain this to my father?' A burly German student was talking to me on one of my visits to Taizé. Son of an evangelical pastor, he had rebelled against his narrow, pietistic upbringing. The worship at Taizé had produced a quite unexpected change. One of the greatest things that Frère Roger and his community have discovered is how to make corporate worship, for thousands of people, the beating heart of their daily lives.

I first met Roger Schutz in 1947 when he was visiting Oxford with Max Thurian, one of the theologians of Taizé. Significantly they gave me as a memento a book about their community worship, *La Joie du Ciel sur la Terre*, the Joy of Heaven on Earth.

Three years later I paid them my first visit at the tiny village of Taizé. We took a train from the Gare de Lyon to Mâcon in Burgundy – what a hot, sticky, sleepless night it was! We changed to a local train for Cluny at some grisly morning hour, saw what little remains of the great abbey there, and then went to Taizé. In the early sunshine we climbed the village street with its cottages of local apricot-coloured stone. First we went into the exquisite medieval village church. It is of course a Roman Catholic church. It had been badly neglected, for this was part of dechristianized France. For years its bell had hardly been rung except for funerals. But now Frère Roger and his companions had been given permission to put the church in order and whitewash its walls. A catholic altar stood at the east end and their reformation communion-table at the chancel step. We climbed on to the top of the village and enjoyed a wide view of the rolling hills of Burgundy patched with woods and vineyards, wheat fields and meadows. Then we went down to the old manor house, which Frère Roger had bought ten years earlier and turned into the community house. All this was years before the Taizé community became famous, and we had a long, long day of unforgettable talk; and already I began to discover the secret, which they have since shared with so many, of living in *l'allégresse de l'aujourd'hui* – the gladness of today.

Roger was born in a manse in the high Juras. His father was a Swiss pastor, his mother, French. His seven sisters chose his name, Roger. It was, he said, a home full of books and full of love. There was strictness about it, though. On its walls among family portraits hung also portraits of the severe Jansenist nuns of Port Royal from seventeenth-century France. Roger was sent away to school and boarded with a poor catholic family near Lausanne. He was a sensitive child, touched by the catholic piety of his new home, but also worried by the lack of charity between protestants and catholics. And then for two years, under the influence of a rationalistic science master, he lost his faith. He came through these troubles in time and went to study theology at Lausanne university to prepare for the ministry. His health was frail; he had to rest a good deal; he took long solitary walks in the country. The recovery through prayer of a beloved sister who had been at death's door brought him certitude, joy and peace. Then to his surprise his fellow-students invited him to become president of the Federation of Christian Students in Lausanne, and at its meetings, which sometimes had prayers rather like a simple monastic office, he spoke for the first time of his hope for a protestant monastic community. A little later he managed to persuade the faculty of theology to accept as the theme for his thesis, *The Monastic Life before St Benedict and its Conformity with the Gospel.* He was convinced that monasticism would give strength and stability to his desires, but a monasticism that bridged the divisions between the churches and was planted in the contemporary world.

His studies finished, he cycled off to France to see his uncle, a French military chaplain near Mâcon, but also to seek this world-in-need, where he could put down the roots of a monastic life. He visited Cluny, not only to see the ruins, but to recall the memory of the great abbot, one of his heroes:

> Peter the Venerable, so human, so concerned with love and unity, capable of actions centuries in advance of his time . . . who, overcoming the prejudices of his time, welcomed and offered a place of retreat to Abelard, when everyone else condemned him.[1]

Roger saw advertised the empty manor house at Taizé. He cycled on, noticing the misery of the half-depopulated village. He asked a poor old woman where there was an inn or café. There was none. She said, 'Come and eat with me,' and when he had explained his plans, pleaded 'Stay with us, we are so lonely.' That settled it for Roger. He bought that derelict, shuttered house. For two years he lived there alone, from the start saying a monastic office three times a day. He gave refuge to Jews and others who were escaping across the border from Nazi-occupied France, only six miles to the north. But while he was on a visit to Switzerland, the Nazis took over the whole of France and the French–Swiss border was now closed against him.

Then he shared an apartment in Geneva with Max Thurian and two other students. This was a kind of proto-community. They organized discussions, and for their worship they were allowed to use a chapel in the Reformed cathedral of St Peter.

With the liberation of France in 1944 the brothers went back to Taizé. They at once made contact with other Christians; Frère Roger was later to write in their rule, 'Have a passion for unity.'[2] They identified themselves with the needs

[1] Roger Schutz, *The Power of the Provisional*, Hodder & Stoughton 1969, pp. 61–2.
[2] *Rule of Taizé* (French and English edition), Les Presses de Taizé 1961, p. 16.

of the place. They started a house for war-orphans with the help of Roger's sister Geneviève. They made friends with German prisoners-of-war – not a popular thing in post-war France. One of the brothers, himself a doctor, practised in the area. They started farming, and by setting up a co-operative with the local farmers they brought prosperity to the region. This again is the spirit of their future rule. 'Open yourself to what is human . . . Be present to your day and age; adapt yourselves to the conditions of the moment.'

Easter 1949 saw a great occasion in the village church when the first seven brothers took their vows for life – or their *engagements*, to use the less legalistic term which they prefer: celibacy, community of goods and acceptance of authority.

In 1951 they began to send small groups of brothers to live for a few years in fraternities. The first went to the neighbouring industrial town, Montceau-les-Mines. I myself visited a fraternity in Marseilles. Another fraternity was in Algeria all through the war there. Others have been dotted about the world from India to South America. The brothers earn their own living, dress and live like their neighbours; but primarily they have gone to be 'a sign of joy and brotherly love among men'. Once a year the whole community comes together to review its strategy and the lives of its scattered fraternities. These are similar to the fraternities of the Little Brothers of Charles de Foucauld. Early on Frère Roger had hoped to link his own community to theirs; but it did not happen. Yet later in 1966 the Taizé brothers were in fact hosts to the Little Brothers and Sisters for the commemoration of the fiftieth anniversary of the death of Charles de Foucauld.

All through these years Taizé was becoming an inspiration to Christians of many churches, but not without opposition. Many in the Reformed Church in France said Taizé was going too fast. Political left-wingers and theological left-wingers still maintain that Taizé is too slow and too traditional. But greater and greater crowds were coming. And their village church was now far too small. Two of the brothers designed a large new church, frankly modern, in concrete. Three groups of young German workers, sixty in each, worked at its construction as a sign of French–German reconciliation after the war. Its exterior is not attractive, but at least it does not spoil the skyline of the hill; when I first saw it, it looked like the hull of a ship ploughing through a rippling field of wheat. The inside, however, is marvellous. There is a feeling of spaciousness and peace. Oblique lighting comes through glowing glass of strong warm colours. The whole building finds its focus – without being overwhelmed – in a simple altar beneath a suspended circle of candles. Under the main church is a crypt for Roman Catholic masses. The great service at the opening of this new church in August 1962 was a highlight, perhaps *the* highlight, of Taizé's directly ecumenical efforts. Yet more was to come. Already in 1959 two brothers had been invited to work at Geneva with the World Council of Churches. In 1963 a small Orthodox centre was founded at Taizé as a result of a visit by Frère Roger to Athenagoras, the Ecumenical Patriarch at Istanbul. Then Frère Roger and Frère Max were invited to be observers throughout the Vatican Council at Rome. While there they had daily at table in their apartment bishops, theologians and fellow-observers. They made special friends with some of the bishops from South America. And so 'Operation Hope', a scheme close to Frère Roger's heart, came into being, and through it large sums of money were sent to the poorest parts of that awakening continent. Roger had always said, 'Love the dispossessed.'

All the time the community was growing in numbers. The great majority were not ministers, but laymen; one was a computer specialist. Soon a few Roman Catholic brothers were officially allowed to join them. 'Who are we?' wrote Frère Roger in 1968:

A small vulnerable community, held up by an irrational hope, the hope of creating harmony between the children of baptism and between men everywhere; a community of seventy men, Christians, called on to do a task which is quite beyond them, and who, in spite of their limited numbers, try to answer every appeal made to them, no matter from which direction.[3]

[3] Roger Schutz, *Violent for Peace*, Darton, Longman & Todd 1968, p. 49.

The student revolt in Paris that May touched Frère Roger deeply. From this time young people came in rapidly-increasing numbers to Taizé, indeed so many that a little later the brothers tore down a wall of the new church and joined on a great circus tent. These young people were following the *dynamique du provisoire* – the power of the provisional – to quote the title of another of Frère Roger's short books. Their chief concern was not with church unity, but with social justice in their own countries and throughout the world. After some hesitation – indeed Roger has confessed to his own fears [4] – it has been decided to have a worldwide Council of Youth in 1974, which is expected to spread over a number of years. Possibly the long Vatican II Council suggested this. Frère Roger indicates the thinking behind this decision.

> After years of good ecumenical work – which brought results – are we not coming to a standstill?

> The idea of a Council of Youth was first born out of a failure: namely, the impasse in which the ecumenical vocation found itself, with so many people brutally rejecting the Church. [5]

The Taizé brothers and these young people are determined that man shall not remain victim to man anywhere in the world, and especially in Asia, Africa and South America. This will mean action, sacrificial action. *Yet they see also the need for prayer – particularly contemplative prayer – to purify their action from all trace of arrogance*. So together they have hammered out their theme: 'Struggle and contemplation to become men and women of communion'. And Frère Roger has also significantly called his recent book *Lutte et Contemplation*, struggle *and* contemplation.

All through the years since 1944 Frère Roger has led a young, forward-looking, closely-knit community – and today he has also an international lay team of young people. But Frère Roger himself is always at the heart of it – one cannot

[4] 'I wonder if we shall have the strength to go ahead in a commitment with the young people. I should like to give up the idea of a council of youth' (entry in his diary 27.1.70): Roger Schutz, *Festival*, SPCK 1974, p. 147.

[5] Ibid., pp. 18, 19.

imagine Taizé without him – that spare, swift-moving figure, a man sensitive to natural beauty, with listening blue eyes, and with, as was said of him when he first settled at Taizé, 'a heart exploding with the love of God and of man'.

But at the centre of his own life and that of the community, and also inspiring thousands of people of the most varied types, has been the worship of the church. Frère Roger often rightly asks: 'Haven't we been discovered and recognized by so many agnostics through our liturgical prayer?'

How can you explain why the worship at Taizé has this influence? The brothers certainly do not try to 'put it across'. It is for them worship offered directly to God. Naturally the effect is partly due to the great numbers of people present: forty or so athletic-looking, white-robed monks and then, surrounding them, masses of people, a thousand or more, from so many countries and mostly under twenty-five. Then you realize that these forms of worship for the eucharist and the other services are really good: they have been drawn up, used daily, tested continually and perfected by this alert community. And very important – visitors to Taizé go to the worship expectant. The bells ring about half an hour beforehand. Young people gradually collect. The brothers come in one or two at a time. Everyone has time to settle down, fascinated by the play of colour through the windows and by the flickering of the circle of candles. There are a few chords from the organ and all join at once in some bold, effective words of praise. Psalms are sung in French to Gelineau tunes with antiphons like choruses. There is good measured reading from the Bible. Hymns are vigorously sung, simultaneously in French, German and English. And there are moments of 'a silence that can be felt', especially as particular needs of the world, the churches and the community are laid before God.

Everything sounds real. Everyone feels free. People stand, kneel, sit, squat or prostrate, as they wish. People sing together without feeling in any sense dragooned. Many feel – and feel increasingly – that they are not so much making an effort as somehow responding, responding to a mysterious reality beyond their grasp, responding to God. They sense that this suits their human nature – that they were made for this. And there is quietness at the end; and then the organ, that unforgettable organ, peals out. As you leave the church, you sense that you must somehow continue to live what you have done. This is, as Christians would say, worship in the Spirit. Curiously enough I have had this very same sense when praying this Taizé office in a small fraternity or with a group of friends. If only we could discover how to have this spirit always, this expectancy, wherever we come together for worship!

For this we need to think more deeply. I wish you could look at the Rule of Taizé. I don't think anyone can read it carefully without being moved. Frère Roger is not very fond of the word 'rule'; he would prefer a less forbidding term. The community asked him to draw up for them the principles of the life they had been living for some years. He did it in his inimitable French. And how modestly he did it.

> If this rule were ever to be regarded as an end in itself and to dispense us from always seeking more and more to discover God's design, the love of Christ and the light of the Holy Spirit, we would be imposing on ourselves a useless burden. Then it would be better never to have written it.[6]

It is a short document. Parts of it of course apply primarily only to members of religious communities, yet the rule as a whole speaks directly to the hearts of all Christians and to seekers after authenticity. Let us now look at what Frère Roger wrote about worship and prayer. He is basing it on experience, his own experience and that of his brothers.

He speaks first of prayer, not as a duty, but as a *joy*. 'I will tell of all thy wondrous deeds, for thou hast turned my mourning into gladness and hast girded me with joy.'

The corporate prayer of the church brings us, he says, into the communion of saints and so with them we 'should give ourselves up to ardent intercessions for all men and for the church'. We need to remember even more that it is with Christ and in Christ that we praise God and pray. So the

[6] *Rule of Taizé*, p. 71. The quotations following are also from the *Rule*.

106

white robe, which the brothers wear for their worship in church, is intended to remind them that as Christians they have 'put on Christ' and their 'whole being has been clothed' with him.

God waits for our collaboration with him in life and also in prayer. What a privilege and responsibility this is! 'The Lord could do without our intercession and our praise. Yet it is the mystery of God, that he should require us, his co-workers, to keep on praying and never to lose heart.'

Our work has to be integrated into our worship if our worship is to become genuine. 'The praise of Christ expressed by the liturgy is effective in so far as it continues to inform the humblest tasks.' For this to be possible, Frère Roger tells us in our worship to 'surrender ourselves to the living Word of God, and let it reach the deepest recesses of our being to take possession not only of our spirit, but also of our body'. This will not always be plain sailing, but we must learn how to go through difficulties and not to become discouraged.

> There will be days when the office is a burden to you. On such occasions know how to offer your body, since your presence itself already signifies your desire, momentarily unrealizable, to praise your Lord. Believe in the presence of Christ with you, even though you feel no tangible response.

As in human friendship and love, we are right to give a sign of affection even if there is not much feeling behind it – it shows at least our desire to love, and sometimes it helps to re-invigorate our affection.

Frère Roger says again and again that communal prayer is not enough and cannot stand alone; personal prayer is absolutely essential. 'Corporate prayer does not dispense us from personal prayer. The one sustains the other. Let us, each day take time to renew our personal intimacy with Jesus.'

And in this personal prayer Frère Roger gives a very important place to simple contemplative prayer. He explains what he means by this in some supplementary directions to the Rule.

> What do we understand by contemplation? Nothing else than that disposition by which our whole being in its totality is seized by the reality of the love of God. When we understand a truth

only on the natural level by our intelligence, we are seized by it, but often only partially. On the other hand we can be seized entirely, including our affections, by supernatural truth, by God's own love. One can say that love here is a touchstone. Contemplation strengthens our love for God. By an intimate union with the love of God contemplation makes us loving also towards our neighbour. If it is authentic, this love of our whole being for Christ cannot but show itself in love towards our neighbour. The love which we bear to others remains the mark of the authenticity of our contemplation.[7]

So he tells us to have done with mere routine and mediocrity in prayer. 'Joyful with infinite gratitude, never fear to precede the dawn to praise and bless and sing Christ your Lord.'

In a characteristic and very revealing passage from one of his books he imagines himself coming before Christ at the last and saying about his community:

What I chiefly loved about it was something which would occur only to a few people. Most people loved Taizé for its open doors and for the way it entered into dialogue with so many men.

Then he adds:

But more than this work of sharing, I look on our waiting, our contemplation, as its greatest quality.[8]

[7] *La Règle de Taizé: directives spirituelles*, Les Presses de Taizé 1962, pp. 128–9 (myown translation).
[8] *Violent for Peace*, p. 37.

Epilogue

We have been watching these dozen men and women developing and growing through their life of prayer. I wonder what is
now striking you most about them. And how much more
intimately you will know them when, as I suggested at the
beginning, you turn to their letters and other writings for
yourself.

What impresses me first is a progressive enrichment, a
growing depth and unity, in their personalities. This is something too profound to define. They are well on the way to
discovering the secret of their own identity, 'hidden', as
Thomas Merton would say, 'in the love and mercy of God'.[1]
Becoming more and more their true selves, they have become
less and less centred on themselves. 'The true self grows',
Teilhard de Chardin found, 'in inverse proportion to the
growth of egoism.'[2] Perhaps they discovered this by learning
to pray *with their whole being*. If they became aware of this
change taking place in themselves, they did not self-cons-
ciously try to measure it or talk about it. One of the Little
Brothers, Carlo Carretto, in his *Letters from the Desert*, is right
to quote Angelo of Foligno, a contemplative of medieval Italy:
'Those who feel God most deeply can say least about him.'
Teilhard also tries to describe this change in his own way. 'The
more the soul's desires are concentrated on God, the more he
will flood into them, penetrate their depths and draw them into
his own *irrestisible simplicity*.'[3]

The flaws and weaknesses of these men and women have by

[1] Thomas Merton, *New Seeds of Contemplation*, Burns & Oates
1962, p. 28.
[2] Teilhard de Chardin, *Hymn of the Universe*, Fontana 1970, p. 111
[3] Ibid., p. 108.

no means entirely gone, though a process of change, a conversion, has really set in. We are 'converted', Thomas Merton writes, 'many times', though one or more of these turnings may stand out significantly, and he adds: 'This endless series of large and small conversions, minor revolutions, leads finally to our transformation in Christ.'[4] This authentic change cannot be humanly engineered. It is the gift of the Spirit of Love to be desired, prepared for and longed for. Our own part is 'humbly to make ourselves ready to accept', Teilhard said – and so did Simone Weil.

I am very conscious of how much further I myself have to go on this road. But when in a reflective mood I look back over the years and remember how as a student I began to take seriously – though I hope not too solemnly – the exploration of praying and living and serving, I realize how much has happened to me. Something has been given and received. There have been, it is true, long periods when I have felt stuck, becalmed in the doldrums, and occasionally I have gone backwards. But I feel like saying with Dag Hammarskjöld:

> For all that has been – Thanks!
> To all that shall be – Yes![5]

I feel I am on the edge of important discoveries – oughtn't I to say, important disclosures? Long since, I have given up trying to model myself on others, however admirable and devoted. Soon perhaps I shall be shown who I, Mark Gibbard, am – and become what I am in the purpose and love of God.

I am no one else. The next thing which strikes me about these men and women of prayer is that they are – they have become – astonishingly different. 'Souls are never dittos,' Friedrich von Hügel wrote to his niece. Genuine prayer is exactly the opposite of being ironed out into a pious uniformity. Each of us has his own personality, his own circumstances, his own spiritual *attrait*. It is within these that our call to respond to God's love comes. Carlo Carretto puts it

[4] Thomas Merton, *Life and Holiness*, Geoffrey Chapman 1968, pp. 158–9.
[5] Dag Hammarskjöld, *Markings*, Faber 1966, p. 87.

with characteristic simplicity: 'Just as no flower is exactly like another flower and no star exactly like another star, so no man is exactly like another man.' And he goes on: 'Since prayer is the relationship between one particular man and God, it is different for every man.'[6]

The man is different, and so is the way. Alan Paton cannot pray as Archbishop Anthony prays. Nor is it much good picking up ideas, one here, one there, and stirring them all up together. We must use our common sense. We may well need 'a guide, philosopher and friend'. How much so many seekers owed to the Abbé Huvelin! But our way can be authentic only if, after adequate testing, it is real *for us*. 'How do you expect to arrive at the end of your journey,' asked Thomas Merton, 'if you take the road to another man's city?'[7] Your responsibility is to explore the way to *your* Tamanrasset.

Then practically all these very different people seem eventually to have found the keystone of their lives in some form or other of contemplative praying. My own vocation takes me about the world; and this growing desire for contemplative praying seems to me in recent years one of the clearest signs of the Spirit – in Johannesburg as well as Jerusalem, in Cambridge as well as Kyoto.

Although in lab and office, in committee and in crowd we can see and meet God in our fellowmen and women, yet also we need times when we can see him and receive him in quietness. This is part of our human nature. Jesus met his Father in his neighbours, but he also needed to find him in a quiet spot in early morning outside the village, on the mountainside at the end of the day and in the solitude of the desert. Carlo Carretto tells you that you need to make your own 'desert', the place where you can 'every now and then leave men and look for solitude to restore, in prolonged silence and prayer, the stuff of your soul'.[8]

For me personally it is a time of silence early in the morning.

[6] Carlo Carretto, *Letters from the Desert*, Darton, Longman & Todd 1972, p. 36.

[7] Merton, *New Seeds of Contemplation*, p. 76.

[8] Carretto, op. cit., p. 73.

I have known this in theory for I do not know how long. But to experience its reality has been my great discovery these last few years. If nowadays I have occasionally to miss it, I don't worry too much, I don't get upset. Yet to miss it is like missing the visit of a friend. Even now this quiet, contemplative time hasn't always the same quality, the same depth – neither have all the meetings with a friend. But frequency builds up intimacy. If you can't find quiet where you live, can't you find a silent church, a park to walk in or a quiet reading-room in a library? Madeleine Delbrêl was sometimes driven to find her time in a metro journey of five stops. You may have to use your ingenuity to find it, but love has its own ingenuity. And I needn't expand the hints I suggested in the chapter on Thomas Merton about the various ways of using that time.

Coming to God in this way quietly and receptively should spill over into our relationships with others and help us to meet them sensitively and receptively. This is so important, for one of the great needs of today is to listen to others – and not with half an ear. Dietrich Bonhoeffer, as we have seen, wrote about this and added its converse: 'He who can no longer listen to his brother will soon be no longer listening to God either.'[9] Through frequent contemplative praying we may be gradually brought to share Teilhard's experience: 'Every presence makes me feel that you are near me; every touch is a touch of your hand; every necessity transmits to me a pulsation of your will.'[10]

Out of this contemplative praying and listening and loving emerges the determination to rid the world, as the brothers and friends of Taizé maintain, of man's injustice to man. Struggle *and* contemplation – here they join hands with Thomas Merton the Trappist with his myriad concerns: 'Action is the stream and contemplation is the spring.'[11]

This kind of contemplative praying is quiet and receptive. But don't get me wrong. It is also paradoxically a long, hard

[9] Dietrich Bonhoeffer, *Life Together*, SCM Press 1965, pp. 75 f.
[10] Teilhard de Chardin, op. cit., p. 139.
[11] Thomas Merton, *No Man is an Island*, Hollis & Carter 1955, p. 61.

road. 'There is no spiritual life', wrote Thomas Merton, 'without persistent struggle and interior conflict.'[12] We advance and explore, even when baffled by our inexplicable moods and doubts. It requires determination. As von Hügel put it in his quaint way, people think that Christianity is a 'not-to-be-grumpy, not-to-be-impatient, not-to-be-violent, a sort of wishy-washy, sentimental affair. Stuff and nonsense. Christianity is not that. Christianity is a heroism.'[13] We need courage to go on, and sometimes to face the world's opposition. Carlo Carretto wrote out of his own experience: 'One has to be courageous not to let oneself be carried along by the world's march. One needs faith and will-power to go *cross-current.*'[14]

We are never alone in our struggle. These men and women of prayer realized that they were together in seeking, praying, worshipping and growing in love. To worship together is not to be drilled into conformity. It is, as we saw so convincingly on the hill of Taizé, minds and hearts gladly together in confession and prayer, in song and praise, in silence and adoration – all in a *milieu* essentially beyond anything we could create for ourselves. This is the church, the mystical Body of Christ; each one of us is part of it, essential to it. Only together, with all God's people stretching across the ranges of space and time, can we, as we have already noticed, discover and grasp 'what is the breadth and length and height and depth of the love of Christ, and to know it, though it is beyond knowledge' (Eph. 3.18-19). Never are we less alone than in our most private prayers. Friedrich von Hügel says with that encouraging good sense of his we so often need: 'Never pray but you realise that you are but one of a countless number of souls, a countless number of stars.'[15] and one also with Jesus our Lord, our great high priest who himself 'ever lives to make intercession for us' – to use again that mysterious image,

[12] Merton, *Life and Holiness*, p. 158.
[13] Friedrich von Hügel, *Letters to a Niece*, J. M. Dent 1928, p. xix.
[14] Carretto, op. cit., p. 130 (my italics).
[15] Von Hügel, op. cit., p. xxiii.

by which the epistle to the Hebrews describes Christ's ceaseless love and concern for us. Bonhoeffer too, you remember, used to emphasize this.

And this fellowship we have with one another in Christ is not a web of uniform, rather prosaic, cool relationships. What marvellous friendships these men and women of prayer made. It was the same with Jesus himself. He had love for all, but there was 'the disciple whom Jesus loved'. So René Voillaume wrote to the Little Brothers: 'We are not to love just platonically and keep it all inside us; we are to love with a love that manifests itself, with a love that comforts and succours, with a love that helps to bear pain, with a love that spreads joy.'[16]

These engaging men and women of prayer were first and last, like true explorers, all-weather men. Frère Roger often in the smiling Burgundy countryside, Teilhard in the icy storms of the Gobi desert, Dag Hammarskjöld in the ferocious United Nations debates, Michel Quoist in his busy parish at Le Havre, Friedrich von Hügel in his sleepless nights at Hampstead – they went on and on.

They all sensed – and we too shall sense, I think, increasingly – 'It is not I who have looked for him. It is He who has looked for me first.'[17]

I have had to find my way – with the prodding encouragement of many friends and the unseen merciful hand of God – through fogs of doubts, through piercing winds of cynicism which found out every cranny, through long sultry days when nothing seemed to happen. But there have been more days than I can count when spring has been in the air.

What is in front of you and of me I do not know. Love calls us on. And doesn't love grow and deepen by our going together in love through all weathers? By this kind of loving we become what we are in the purpose of God for service in the world.

So it is in prayer.

'We are what we pray.'[18]

[16] René Voillaume, *Seeds of the Desert*, Burns & Oates 1955, p. 323.
[17] Carretto, op. cit., p. 37.
[18] Ibid., p. 35.

For Further Reading

Chapter 1

Elizabeth Hamilton, *The Desert My Dwelling Place*, Hodder & Stoughton, 1968
  Biography of Charles de Foucauld and account of the Fraternities.

J. F. Six, *Spiritual Autobiography of Charles de Foucauld*, Anthony Clarke Books 1972
  Selection of Charles de Foucauld's writings.

Carlo Carretto, *Letters from the Desert*, Darton, Longman & Todd 1972
  A Little Brother's meditations in the Sahara.

René Voillaume, *Seeds of the Desert*, Burns & Oates 1955 and Anthony Clarke Books 1972
  On the spirituality of the Little Brothers.

René Voillaume, *Brothers of Men*, Darton, Longman & Todd 1966
  Letters to the Little Brothers.

René Voillaume, *The Need for Contemplation*, Darton, Longman & Todd, 1972
  A way towards contemplation today.

Full bibliography and other information from Jesus Caritas Secretariat, 21 Jubilee Place, London SW3 3TD.

Chapter 2

Friedrich von Hügel, *The Life of Prayer*, J. M. Dent 1927
  The essence of his teaching on prayer.

P. Franklin Chambers (ed.), *Selected Writings*, Fontana 1964
  Extracts from von Hügel's personal, philosophical and religious writings.

Gwendolen Greene (ed.), *Letters from Baron Friedrich von Hügel to a Niece*, J. M. Dent 1928
  Six years of down-to-earth spiritual direction.

Douglas V. Steere (ed.), *Spiritual Counsels and Letters of Baron Friedrich von Hügel*, Darton, Longman & Todd 1964
  More examples of his spiritual direction.

J. P. Whelan, *The Spirituality of Friedrich von Hügel*, Collins 1971
  A scholarly thesis with full bibliography.

M. de la Bedoyère, *The Life of Baron von Hügel*, J. M. Dent 1951

Chapter 3

Simone Weil, *Waiting on God*, Routledge & Kegan Paul 1951; Fontana 1959
  A useful selection of her writings, mostly autobiographical.

Richard Rees, *Simone Weil: Seventy Letters*, OUP 1965
  Letters showing her more human side.

David Anderson, *Simone Weil*, SCM Press 1971
  A clear, short life of Simone Weil, with a bibliography.

Madeleine Delbrêl, *Nous Autres, Gens des Rues*, Editions du Seuil, Paris 1966
  Much biographical material.

Madeleine Delbrêl, *Joie de Croire*, Editions du Seuil, Paris 1969
  Advice on prayer.

Bibliography and information about her fraternity from Association des Amis de Madeleine Delbrêl, 6 rue Philbert Lucot, Paris 13.

Chapter 4

Dietrich Bonhoeffer, *Letters and Papers from Prison*, The Enlarged Edition (which also includes a short essay by his fiancée), SCM Press 1971

Dietrich Bonhoeffer, *Life Together*, SCM Press 1954, 1965
  The life of fellowship and prayer at the Finkenwalde seminary.

Dietrich Bonhoeffer, *The Cost of Discipleship*, SCM Press 1959
  An example of his expounding the New Testament.

Eberhard Bethge, *Dietrich Bonhoeffer*, Collins 1970
  His definitive biography of over 850 pages – even so slightly shortened from the German original.

Mary Bosanquet, *The Life and Death of Dietrich Bonhoeffer*, Hodder & Stoughton 1968
  A perceptive, shorter biography.

André Dumas, *Dietrich Bonhoeffer: Theologian of Reality*, SCM Press 1971
  An analysis of his theology, set in the context of his life; with a bibliography.

Chapter 5

Pierre Teilhard de Chardin, *Letters from a Traveller*, Collins 1962; Fontana 1967
  A good way to begin reading Teilhard.

Pierre Teilhard de Chardin, *Le Milieu Divin*, Collins 1969; Fontana 1964
  The heart of his teaching on prayer.

Pierre Teilhard de Chardin, *The Phenomenon of Man*, Collins 1959; Fontana 1965
  His master work.

Vernon Sproxton, *Teilhard de Chardin*, SCM Press 1971
  A short biography to start on.

J. V. Kopp, *Teilhard de Chardin Explained*, Mercier Press, Cork 1964
  A brief introduction to his thought.

Robert Speaight, *Teilhard de Chardin*, Collins 1967
  Biography, brief estimates of his writings, and bibliography.

Further information from the Teilhard Centre for the Future of Man, 3 Cromwell Place, London SW7 2JE.

Chapter 6

Dag Hammarskjöld, *Markings*, Faber, 1964; paperback ed. 1966
  His spiritual diary.

H. P. van Dusen, *Dag Hammarskjöld: a Biographical Interpretation*, Faber 1967
  Invaluable, as it puts the paragraphs of *Markings* into their context.

Alan Paton, *Kontakion For You Departed*, Jonathan Cape 1969
Largely autobiographical.

Alan Paton, *Instrument of Thy Peace*, Fontana 1969
His reflections on the prayer of St Francis of Assisi.

Chapter 7

Thomas Merton, *Elected Silence*, Hollis & Carter 1949;
Anthony Clarke Books 1961
Autobiography; in later life he himself criticized a good deal of this book.

Thomas Merton, *Seeds of Contemplation*, Burns & Oates 1949

Thomas Merton, *New Seeds of Contemplation*, Burns & Oates 1962
Essays on prayer and contemplation.

Thomas Merton, *Conjectures of a Guilty Bystander*, Burns & Oates 1968
Selections from his journal 1956–65.

Thomas Merton, *Contemplative Prayer*, Darton, Longman & Todd 1973
His most mature writing on prayer, with an important foreword by Douglas V. Steere.

The Asian Journal of Thomas Merton ed. from his original notebooks by Naomi Burton, Brother Patrick Hart & James Laughlin, SPCK 1974
His last journey.

J. J. Higgins, *Merton's Theology of Prayer*, Cistercian Publications, Spencer, Mass. 1971
Analysis of his spirituality, with 24 pages of bibliography.

Chapter 8

Michel Quoist, *Prayers of Life*, Gill & Macmillan 1963
Free-form prayers based on daily life.

Michel Quoist, *The Christian Response*, Gill & Macmillan 1965
Michel Quoist, *Christ is Alive!*, Gill and Macmillan 1971
Michel Quoist, *Meet Christ and Live!*, Gill and Macmillan 1973
These three books give the outlook and theology which lie behind *Prayers of Life*.

Chapter 9

Anthony Bloom, *Living Prayer*, Darton, Longman & Todd 1966

Anthony Bloom, *School for Prayer*, Darton, Longman & Todd 1970
> An introduction to Archbishop Anthony Bloom and his teaching on prayer.

Anthony Bloom, *God and Man*, Darton, Longman & Todd 1971; Hodder & Stoughton 1974
> Includes two TV interviews, 'The Atheist and the Archbishop', with Marghanita Laski and Anthony Bloom.

Anthony Bloom, *Meditations on a Theme*, A. R. Mowbray 1972

R. M. French, *The Way of a Pilgrim*, SPCK 1972: with an introduction by Anthony Bloom
> An insight into Eastern Orthodox spirituality.

Chapter 10

Rule of Taizé (French and English edition), Les Presses de Taizé 1961
> Indispensable for the spirit of Taizé and its worship.

Roger Schutz, *Festival*, SPCK 1974
> Extracts from Frère Roger's diary of 1969–70.

Roger Schutz, *Struggle and Contemplation*, SPCK 1974.
> A sequel to *Festival*.

Peter Moore, *Tomorrow is Too Late*, A. R. Mowbray 1970
> Account of Taizé by an Anglican.

Jean-Marie Paupert, *Taizè et L'Eglise de demain*, Fayard, Paris 1967
> This gives the 'feel' of Taizé, and in the postface has a probing dialogue on their worship.

Taizé 1974: Dare to Live, SPCK 1973
> Young people's reflections in preparation for the Taizé Council of Youth.

Further information and bibliography from 71460 Taizé-Communauté, France.

Index